Human Body

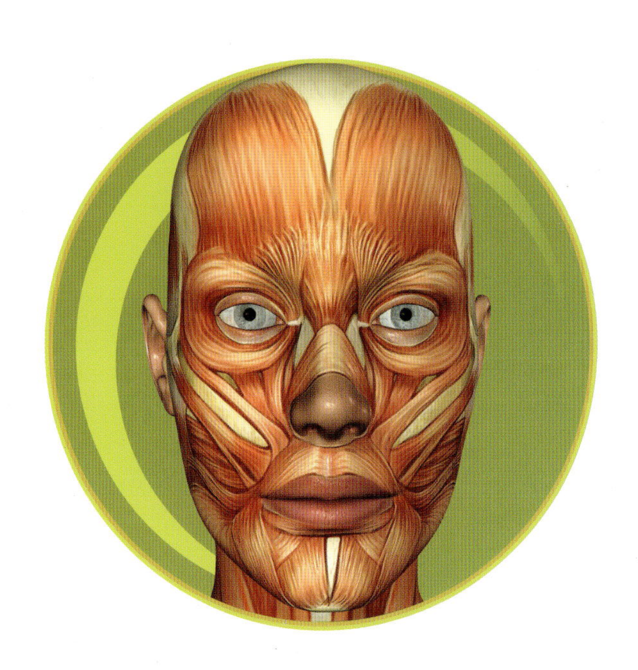

LIVE. LEARN. DISCOVER.

Bath • New York • Singapore • Hong Kong • Cologne • Delhi • Melbourne

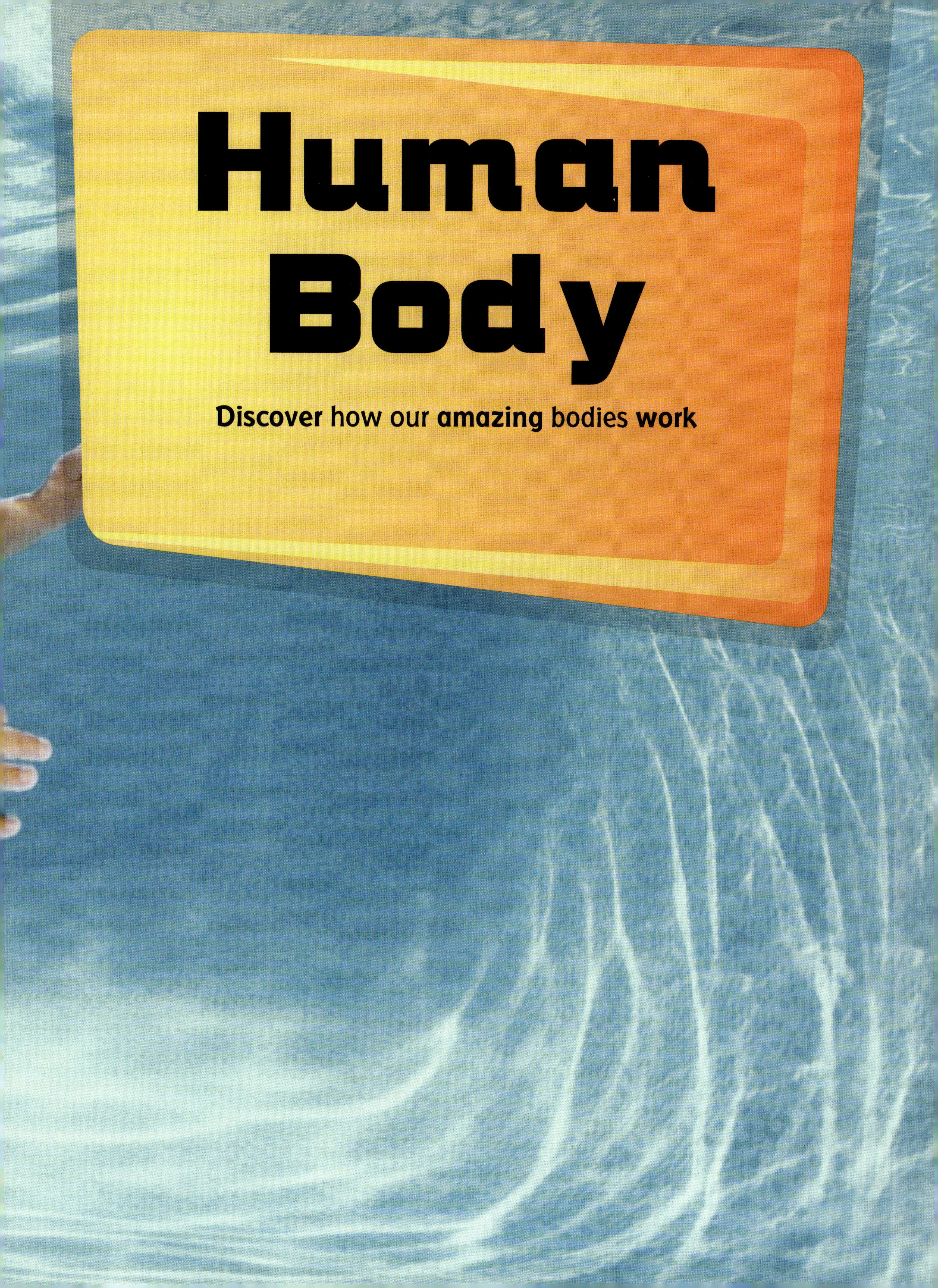

Human Body

Discover how our amazing bodies work

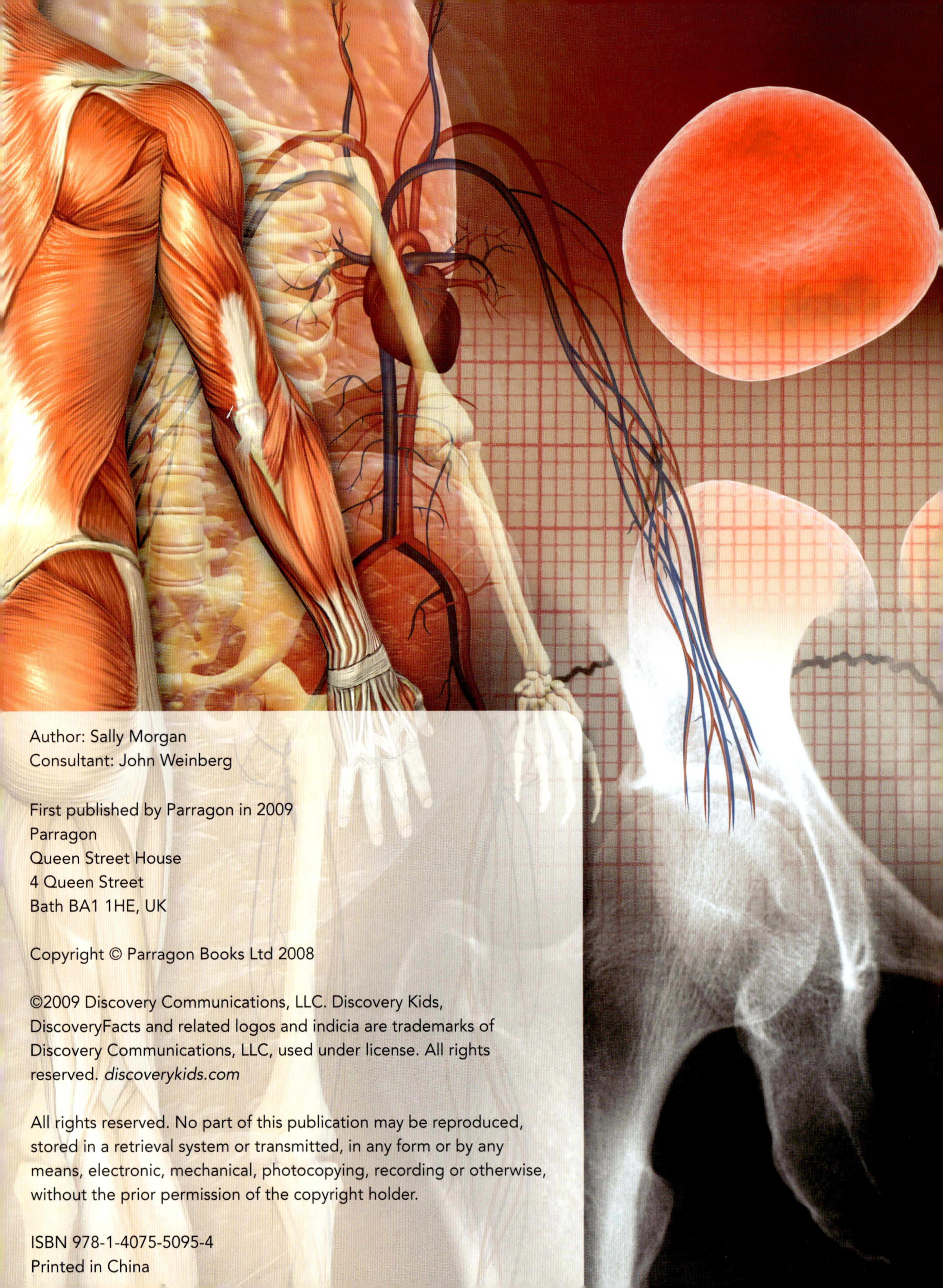

Author: Sally Morgan
Consultant: John Weinberg

First published by Parragon in 2009
Parragon
Queen Street House
4 Queen Street
Bath BA1 1HE, UK

ISBN 978-1-4075-5095-4
Printed in China

Contents

Skin, hair, and nails 6

Bones, joints, and muscles 19

Lungs and breathing 31

Heart and blood 45

Food and digestion 57

Brain and nerves 71

The senses 83

Index 93

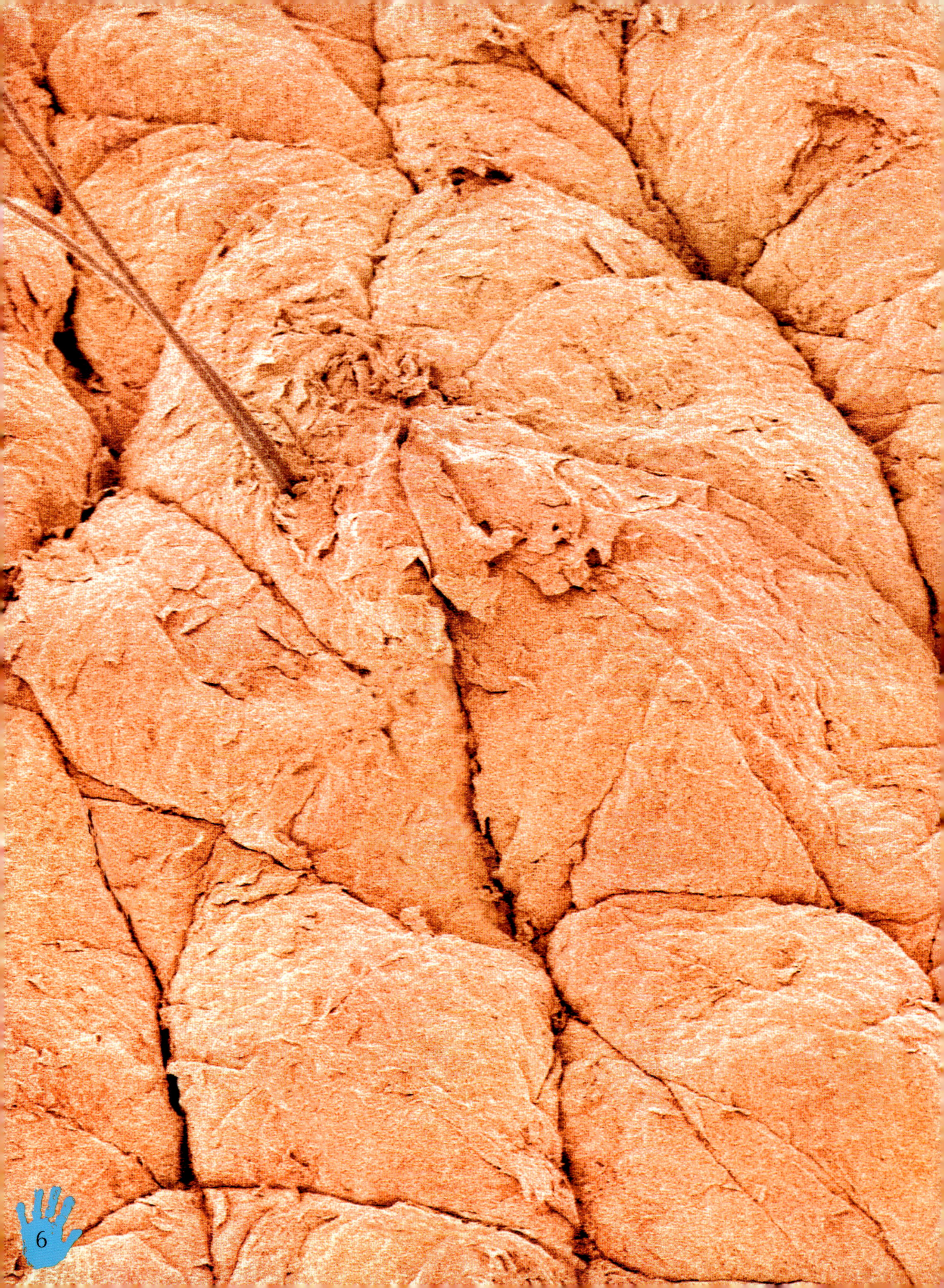

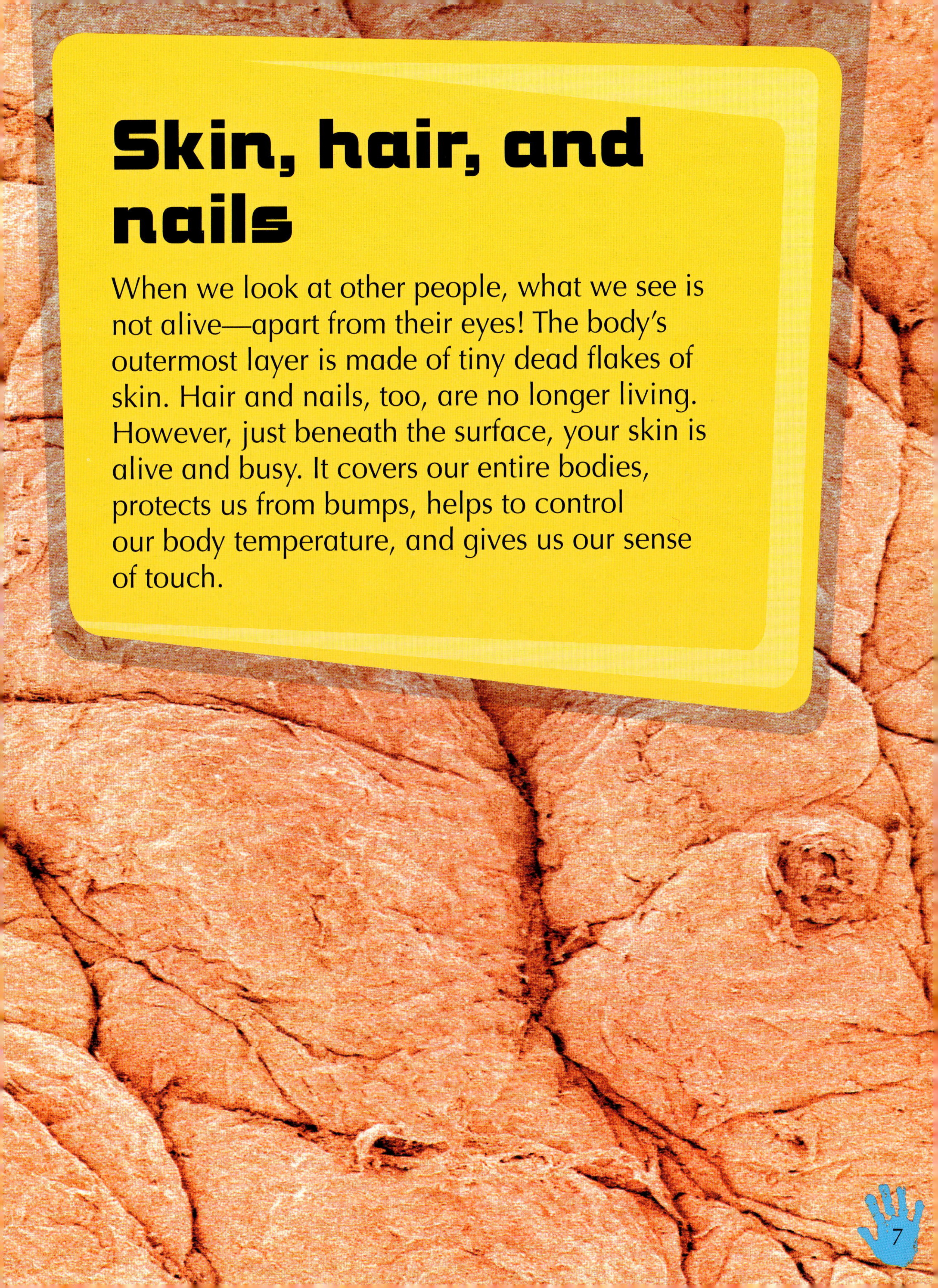

Skin, hair, and nails

When we look at other people, what we see is not alive—apart from their eyes! The body's outermost layer is made of tiny dead flakes of skin. Hair and nails, too, are no longer living. However, just beneath the surface, your skin is alive and busy. It covers our entire bodies, protects us from bumps, helps to control our body temperature, and gives us our sense of touch.

A closer look at skin

Your skin forms a tough barrier to keep out dirt, germs, and harmful rays from the sun. It also stops your body from losing important fluids, salts, and other substances. The skin, hair, and nails together are known as the body's integumentary, or covering, system.

Skin's outer layer

Look through a microscope and you will see that skin has two layers. The outermost or upper layer is called the epidermis. This is made up mostly of dead skin cells and it provides the main protection. The epidermis varies in thickness on different parts of the body. Wherever there is more wear, such as on the soles of the feet, friction and rubbing cause the epidermis to grow thicker.

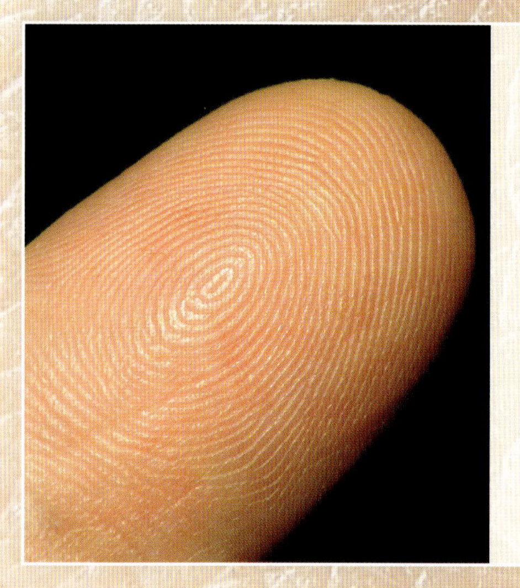

Fingerprints

The tips of your fingers have ridges of skin forming patterns of swirls, curls, and loops, known as fingerprints. They help the skin to grip well. Every person has a unique pattern of fingerprints. A few animals, such as koalas, have fingerprints, too.

The inner layer

Beneath the epidermis is the lower layer of skin, which is called the dermis. The dermis is very flexible because it has tiny strands or fibers that allow it to stretch easily and then spring back into shape. The dermis also holds the roots of your skin's hair (see right).

DiscoveryFact™

Every year, about 4 1/2 pounds of your skin is rubbed off and flakes away. That's enough to fill a bucket!

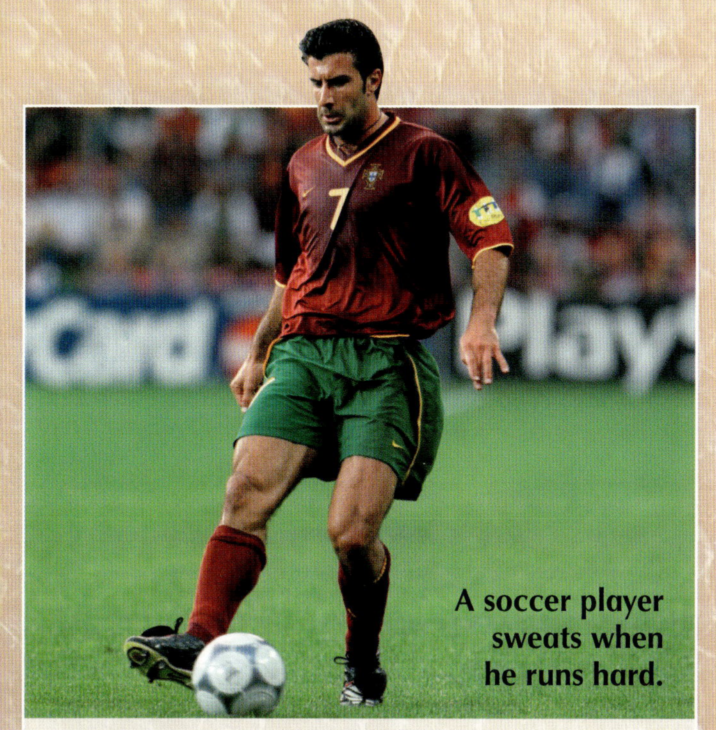
A soccer player sweats when he runs hard.

Cooling sweat

When your body gets hot, your skin releases sweat. This is called perspiration. The sweat flows out onto the skin's surface and draws heat from the body as it evaporates (turns into vapor). Even when cool, your body still makes small amounts of sweat, which is known as insensible perspiration.

Did you know?

- The total skin area of an average adult body would, if laid out flat, cover nearly 21 1/2 square feet.
- The weight of an adult's skin is around 6 1/2 pounds.
- The thin skin on the eyelids is only 1/5 inch thick.
- The skin on the soles of the feet can measure more than 1/5 inch thick.

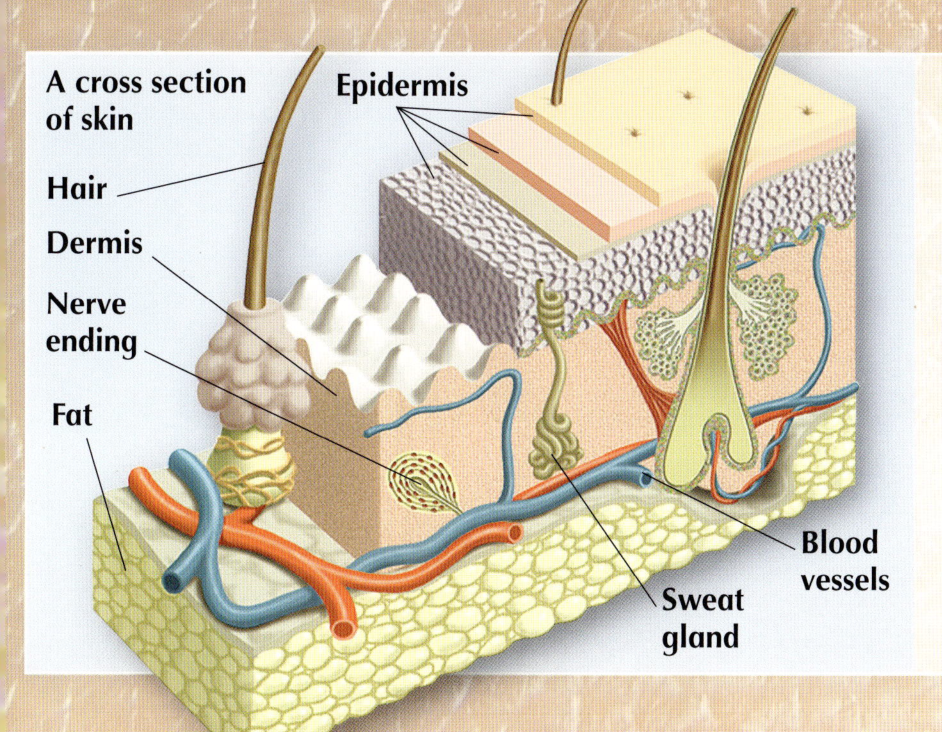

Under the surface

The dermis layer of the skin is packed with millions of microscopic parts, such as blood vessels, nerve endings for touch, pain, and temperature (see page 12), and glands that make sweat. Just under the dermis is a layer of soft fat, which acts like a cushion to absorb bumps.

Skin color

People's skin color varies, even within the same family. The basic color of our skin is inherited from our parents, but it gets darker if we go out in the sun frequently.

DiscoveryFact™

There are more than 10,000 melanocytes in an area of skin about the size of a fingernail. This number is about the same for everybody. In people with darker skin, the melanocytes are more active and make more melanin.

Melanin

Skin color comes from tiny particles of pigment (a type of dark substance) called melanin. These particles are made by cells called melanocytes, which lie at the base of the epidermis. The melanocytes give their melanin to the surrounding skin cells. Strong sunlight makes the skin produce more melanin and go darker, which is known as a suntan.

Make sure your skin is protected by rubbing in sunscreen regularly.

Sunscreen

Protecting the skin against strong sunlight is very important because it reduces the risk of skin cancer. Sunscreen lotions and creams filter out the harmful rays, especially UV-B (ultraviolet B). Such rays can pass through thin clouds, so you should rub in sunscreen protection even on hazy summer days.

No color

Very rarely, the skin produces little or no coloring substances. The result is an overall white or pale pink coloration of skin, hair, and eyes, known as albinism. This can happen in animals, such as this peacock (right), and in humans, too.

An albino peacock

Sunburn

The higher amounts of melanin in suntanned skin help to protect the skin and body parts beneath from the sun's rays. If strong sunlight shines on pale skin, it can cause painful sunburn, with redness and blisters forming in just an hour or two.

Group of children with different skin colors

Pigment cells

Melanocytes have long, fingerlike extensions, called dendrites. These dendrites produce tiny particles of melanin. The melanin passes into surrounding cells, which then begin their journey to the surface.

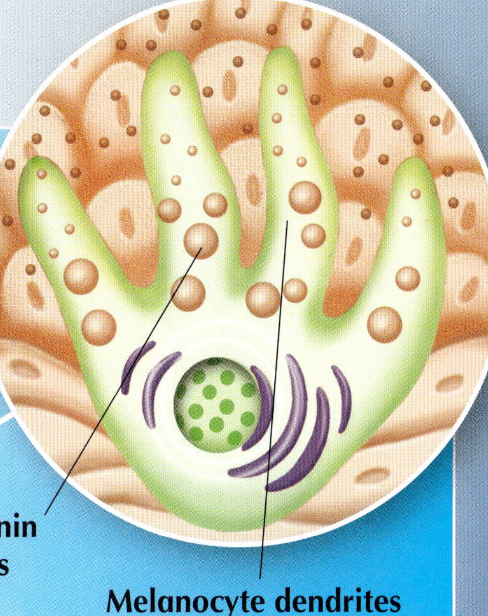

Cuts and wounds

The skin is your body's first defense against knocks and blows. Small cuts, scratches, and bruises are common and the skin can repair these small wounds by itself. Bigger injuries may need help, such as stitches to close the wound and a bandage covering.

Sealing the wound

As soon as skin is injured, blood leaks from its tiny vessels. The vessels narrow to reduce the amount of blood loss. The damage also causes substances in the blood to form microscopic strands or fibers, called fibrin. These tangle together and trap platelets, which are small sticky cells found in blood (see pages 52–53). The fibers and platelets build up and trap red blood cells, forming a sticky lump called a clot. The clot stops more blood from leaking out and prevents dirt and germs from getting in.

An ice hockey player with a black (bruised) eye

Bruises

A bruise is blood that leaks from damaged blood vessels under the skin. It can be red, blue, or purple at first, but then changes to yellow as the blood slowly breaks down.

How skin heals

As a blood clot starts to form, white blood cells leak out of nearby blood vessels and enter the wound to deal with any possible infection. Once a hard scab has formed, dividing skin cells in the epidermis form a new layer of skin.

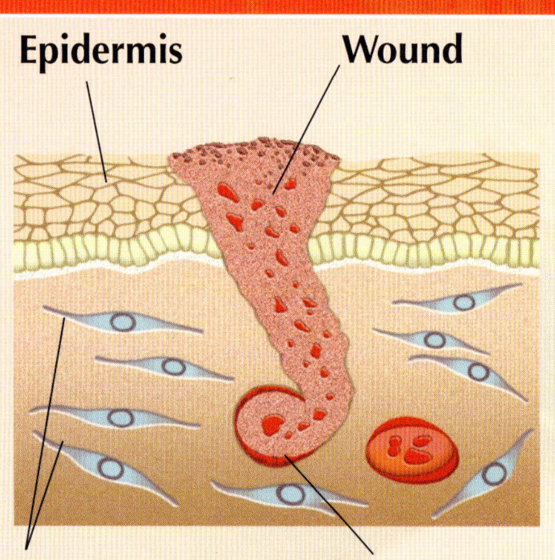

1. Damage caused to blood vessel

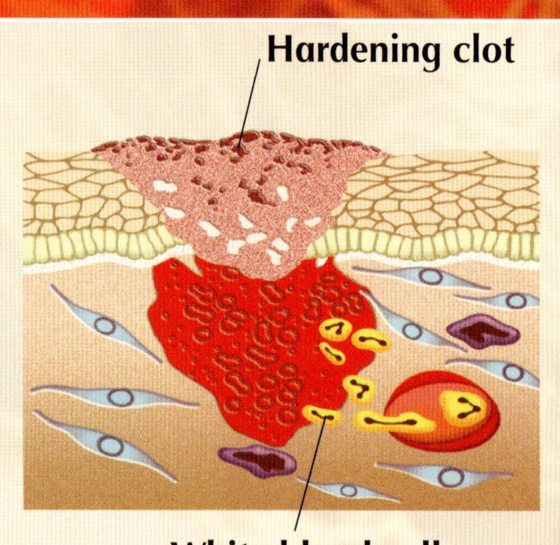

2. Blood clot starts to harden

As good as new

Gradually, the clot hardens and dries into a tough covering known as a scab. Underneath, the skin's damaged edges begin to grow together, slowly forming new skin and closing the cut. Finally, the dry scab falls off, and the repair is complete. A big cut or wound may leave an area of skin that is slightly thicker and a different color. This is called a scar.

Strands of fibrin (shown in yellow) trap red blood cells and platelets to form a clot.

Did you know?

- Some people are born lacking a substance in their blood that helps the blood to clot after an injury. If they cut themselves, the blood doesn't clot and keeps flowing. This condition is called hemophilia.
- In 1965, scientists discovered which clotting substances were missing. Today, hemophilia can be treated with injections of the missing substances.

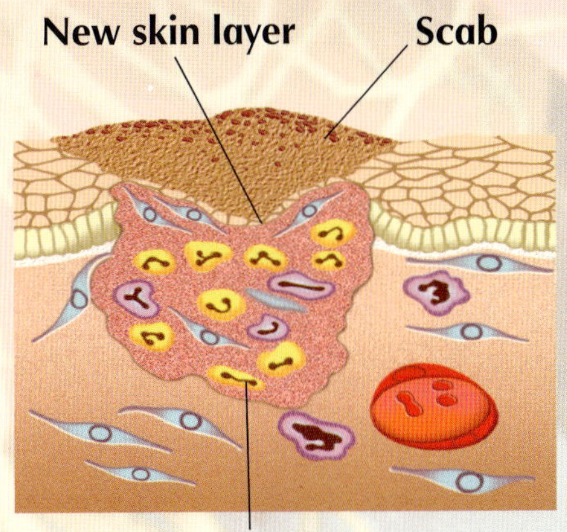

3. New skin layer forms

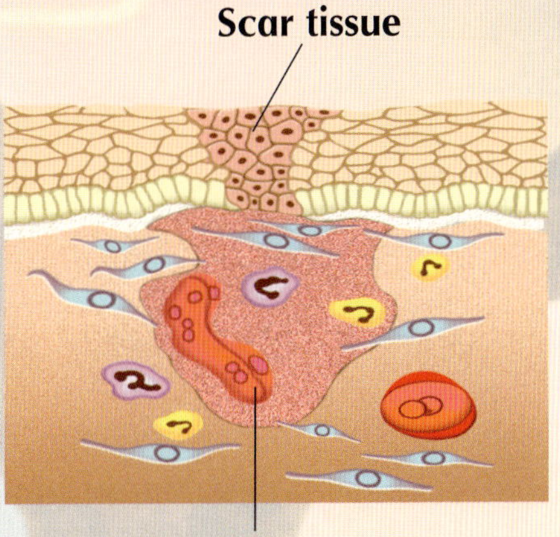

4. Scar tissue forms

DiscoveryFact™

When skin is repairing a big cut, it produces a million extra microscopic cells every hour to heal the gap.

How hair grows

Hairs can look shiny and smooth or rough and crinkled, but they can never "glow with life" because they are dead! The only living part of a hair is its base, from where it grows and gets longer.

In the pits

A hair grows from a hair follicle. The hair lengthens as new microscopic cells add to its base or root. The cells quickly become hard and flat, like dermis cells (see page 12). The hair cells stick together to form a scaly-looking rod that slowly pushes upward out of the follicle.

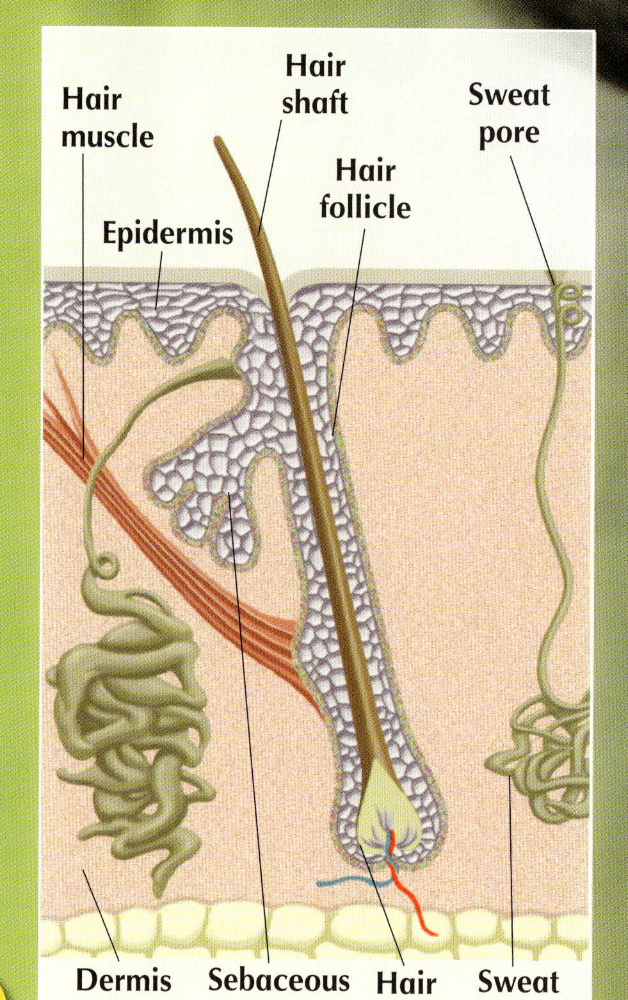

Hair follicle

The hair follicle is a fold in the epidermis that leads down into the dermis. The hair shaft grows up the follicle to the surface. The hair is linked to a muscle, which can pull the follicle so that the hair stands up.

DiscoveryFact™

In most people, if the head hairs are not cut, they will grow to about 5 feet long before falling out naturally. But some people have unusual hair that can grow longer than 20 feet!

Hair shaft

Under a microscope, you can see the edges of the stuck-together flat cells on a hair shaft. Hair thickness varies from less than $^{1}/_{1,000}$ inch to more than $^{1}/_{250}$ inch across.

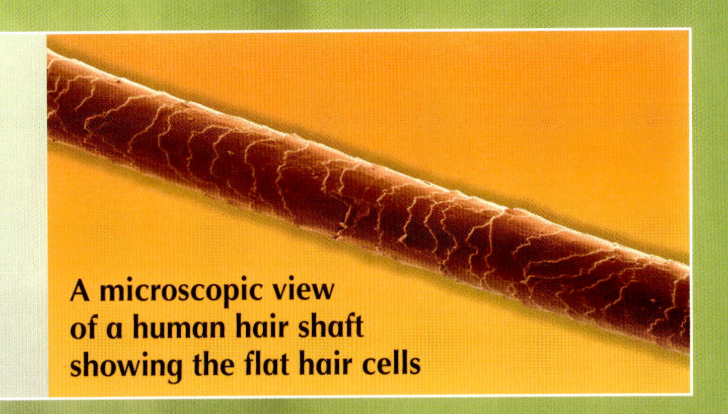

A microscopic view of a human hair shaft showing the flat hair cells

Skin's natural oil

Next to each hair follicle is a tiny lump-like part called a sebaceous gland. This makes a slightly greasy substance, called sebum, which is skin's natural oil. It oozes up to the skin's surface and spreads out. Sebum keeps skin soft and supple. It also helps to repel water and kill germs.

A man with hair styled by cutting it and using chemicals to make it spike up

Natural hair

Hair can be straight, wavy, curly, or frizzy. The natural style of your hair depends upon the cross section of the thousands of hairs on your head, which can be almost circular or nearly flat.

A variety of natural hair styles

Did you know?

- **Head hairs grow by about $^{1}/_{8}$ inch each week.**
- **Fine, fair hair grows more slowly than thick, dark hair.**
- **After a hair falls out, the follicle "rests" for up to six months.**
- **Then a new hair starts to grow from the same follicle.**

Fingernails and toenails

Nails are very useful, not just for a quick scratch. They help to make the backs of the fingertips stiff rather than floppy. This lets you judge the pressure of your grip more precisely, so you can pick up a delicate flower or a tiny pin.

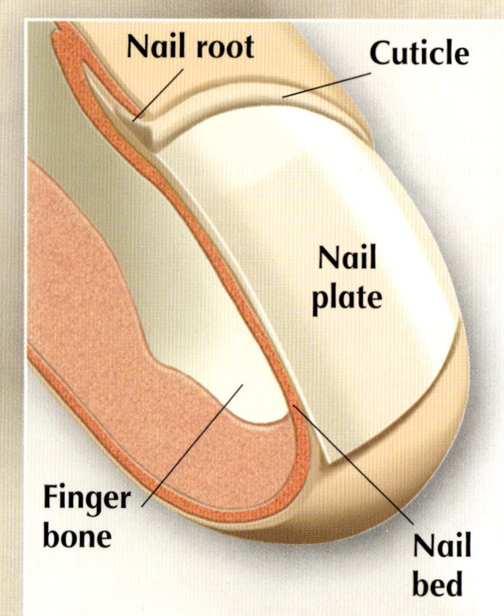

Nail structure

The nail plate is a curved slab of keratin, which sits on the nail bed. Along its bottom edge is the sensitive skin of the nail lateral border, often called the cuticle or "quick." Most people trim their nails but some people let them grow and grow until they reach more than 27 1/2 inches long!

How nails grow

Like hairs and the outer layer of skin, nails are made of keratin. The main sheet, or plate, of the nail is dead. It is only alive at its root, which is hidden under the skin of the finger or toe. As the nail lengthens from its root, it slides along the nail bed, toward the tip of the finger or toe.

The tip of the nail that overhangs the nail bed is called the free edge.

Faster and slower

Most nails grow about $1/2$ inch each month. Fingernails grow slightly faster than toenails, and all nails grow faster in warm weather than in cold conditions. A bang or blow to the nail base can cause damage to the part of the nail forming there. This can create a ridge or lump, which grows along with the rest of the nail, until it can be cut away.

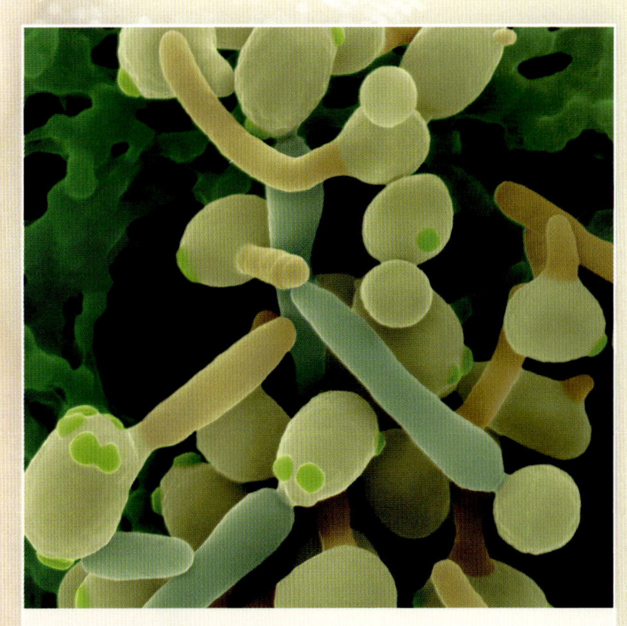

Nail fungus

Candida albicans (above) is a type of fungus that is fairly common on the human body. Sometimes, however, this fungus can grow out of control and cause infections. This can lead to painful inflammation around the nails, while the nails themselves can become ridged and brittle and change color to green or yellow.

A lion's claws are usually pulled inside its paws so that they stay sharp.

Paws and claws

Keratin is also the substance that forms animal claws. Unlike your fingernails, a lion's claws are sharpened to a point so that they can tear through and grip any prey.

Nails and grip

- Before you trim your nails, carefully try to pick up a pin. It should be easy.
- Trim your nails neatly and wash your hands thoroughly.
- Try to pick up the pin again. Short nails, and dry skin without slightly sticky sebum oil, make it much harder.

Quick Quiz

Are these sentences TRUE or FALSE? Place the correct sticker in the box.

1. The thin skin on the eyelids is only 1/5 inch thick.
2. Everybody has the same fingerprint.
3. An albino is someone with black hair.
4. A bruise is blood that leaks from damaged blood vessels.
5. Fine, fair hair grows more slowly than thick, dark hair.

Find the stickers to finish the diagrams.

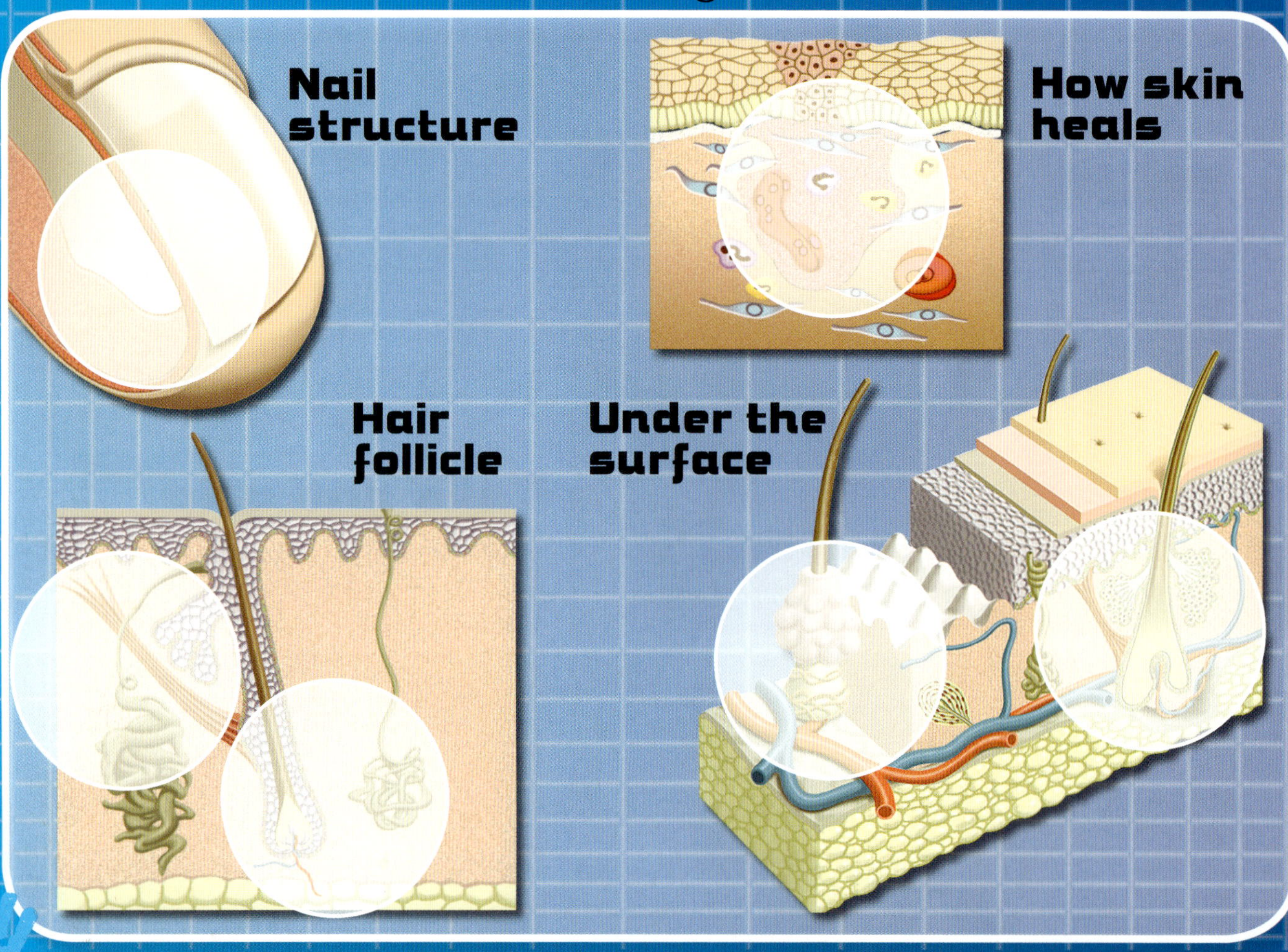

ANSWERS: 1 – T, 2 – F, 3 – F, 4 – T, 5 – T

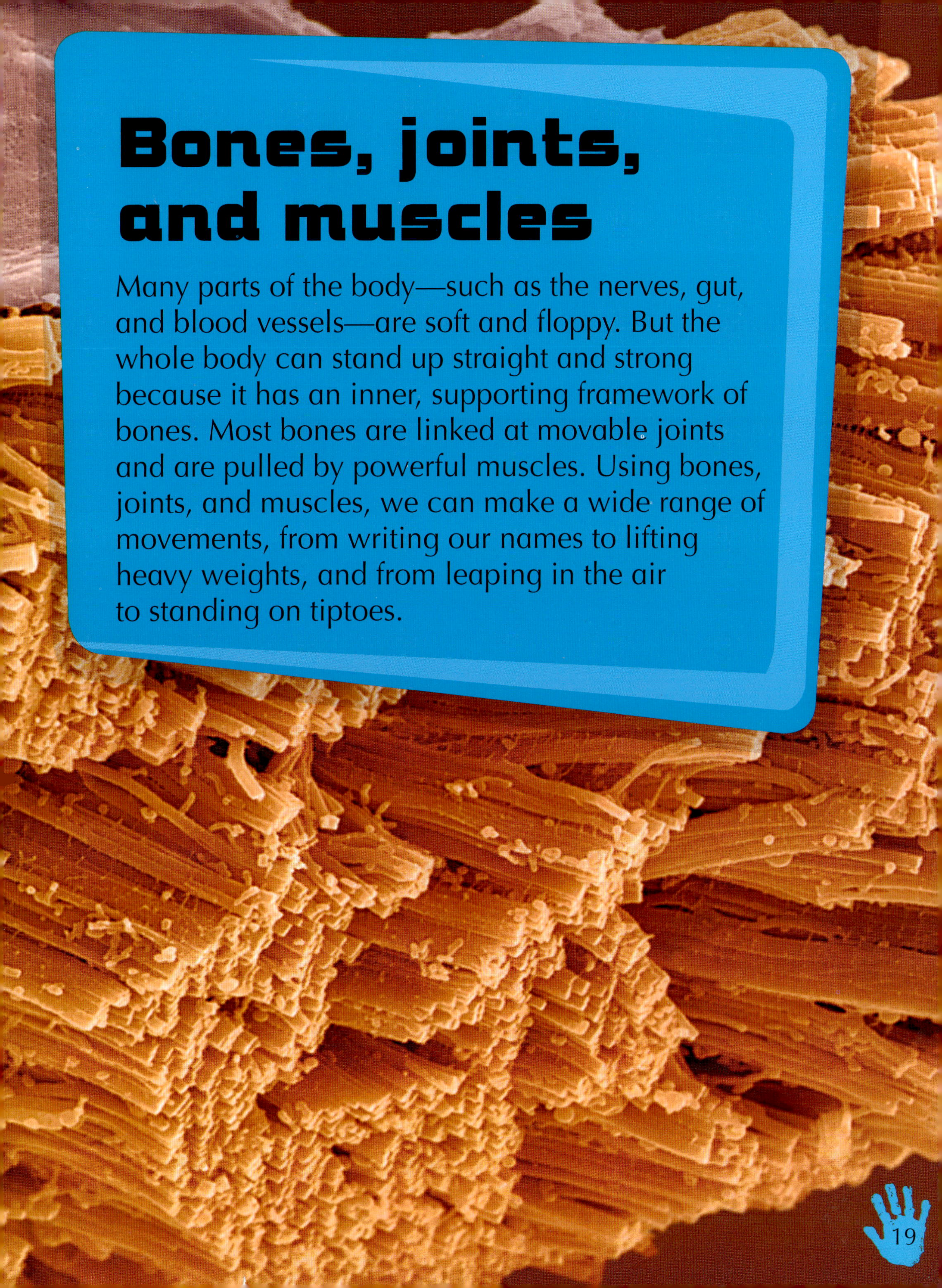

Bones, joints, and muscles

Many parts of the body—such as the nerves, gut, and blood vessels—are soft and floppy. But the whole body can stand up straight and strong because it has an inner, supporting framework of bones. Most bones are linked at movable joints and are pulled by powerful muscles. Using bones, joints, and muscles, we can make a wide range of movements, from writing our names to lifting heavy weights, and from leaping in the air to standing on tiptoes.

The skeleton

All the bones together are called the skeletal system, or skeleton. Each bone is a certain size and shape, depending on its job. The arm and leg bones are long and tube-shaped. The shoulder and hip bones are wide and flat to hold and anchor muscles.

Guarding the body

Some bones are protective. The dome of the skull bone at the top of the head protects the brain. The ribs in the chest are like the bars of a cage, guarding the soft lungs and pumping heart. The bowl-like shape of the hip bone protects the soft organs of the lower body.

Upper skull (*cranium*)
Lower jaw (*mandible*)
Neck bones (*cervical vertebrae*)
Shoulder blade (*scapula*)
Collarbone (*clavicle*)
Breastbone (*sternum*)
Ribs (*costae*)
Upper arm bone (*humerus*)
Forearm bones (*ulna, radius*)
Hip bone (*pelvis*)
Finger bones (*phalanges*)
Lower backbones (*lumbar vertebrae*)

Did you know?

- The human skeleton has a total of 206 bones.
- There are 29 bones in the head and face, 26 in the back, and 25 in the chest.
- There are 63 bones in the shoulders, arms, hands, and fingers and 62 bones in the hips, legs, feet, and toes.

These people are using their bones and muscles to push a car.

Ready, steady, push

As we push, muscles hold the skeleton and keep it in position, allowing the bones to take the strain. The legs, back, and arms transfer a forward force to the object being pushed.

Robert Wadlow in 1938

Outsized skeleton

The height of the body depends on the size of the skeleton. The tallest person ever, at almost 9 feet, was Robert Wadlow (1918–1940) of the United States. His thigh bone alone was half the height of an average adult.

MAIN BONES OF THE HUMAN SKELETON

Kneecap (*patella*)

Lower leg bones (*fibula*, *tibia*)

Foot bones (*tarsals*)

Thigh bone (*femur*)

Toe bones (*phalanges*)

DiscoveryFact™

The longest bone is the femur, or thigh bone, which forms 1/4 of the body's height. The shortest bone is the stirrup in the ear.

Not too stiff

Bones are hard, but they are not completely rigid, or stiff, especially in children and young people. This means they can bend slightly to take great strain rather than cracking or snapping. Bones are light yet tough—weight for weight, they are stronger than most metals and high-tech plastics. And bones can do what metals and plastics cannot—if they are damaged, they can repair themselves.

Smallest bones

The smallest bones are the hammer, anvil, and stirrup inside the ear. Each of these tiny bones is about 1/5 inch long. They are known as the auditory ossicles and they carry sound from the eardrum to the innermost part of the ear, the cochlea.

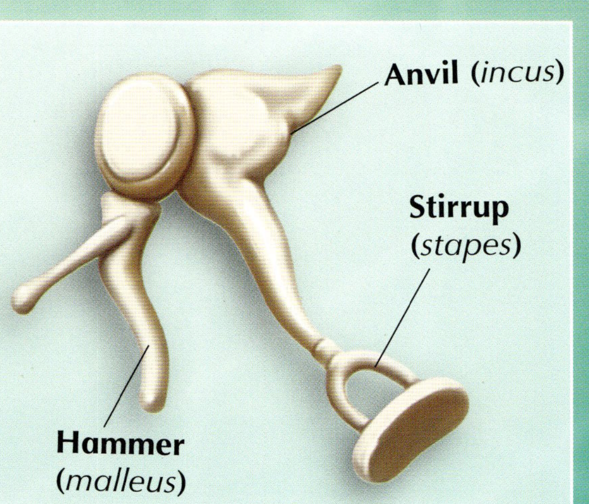

Inside a bone

A typical bone is not solid. The strongest part is the outer layer called compact bone. Inside this is a layer known as cancellous bone, with holes like a sponge. And inside this, in the middle of the bone, is a soft, jellylike substance called bone marrow.

Magnified view of haversian systems in compact bone

Haversian systems

Compact bone is made of thousands of tiny rod-like parts called haversian systems. At the middle of each of these is a hole carrying blood vessels and nerves. Each hole is surrounded by circular layers of bone, called lamellae.

Fibers and minerals

Bone tissue contains a network of tiny fibers made of a substance called collagen. It also contains hard crystals of the minerals calcium carbonate and calcium phosphate. These crystals are scattered among the collagen fibers. The fibers are flexible and allow the bones to bend slightly, while the minerals make the bones very hard.

CUTAWAY VIEW OF A LONG BONE

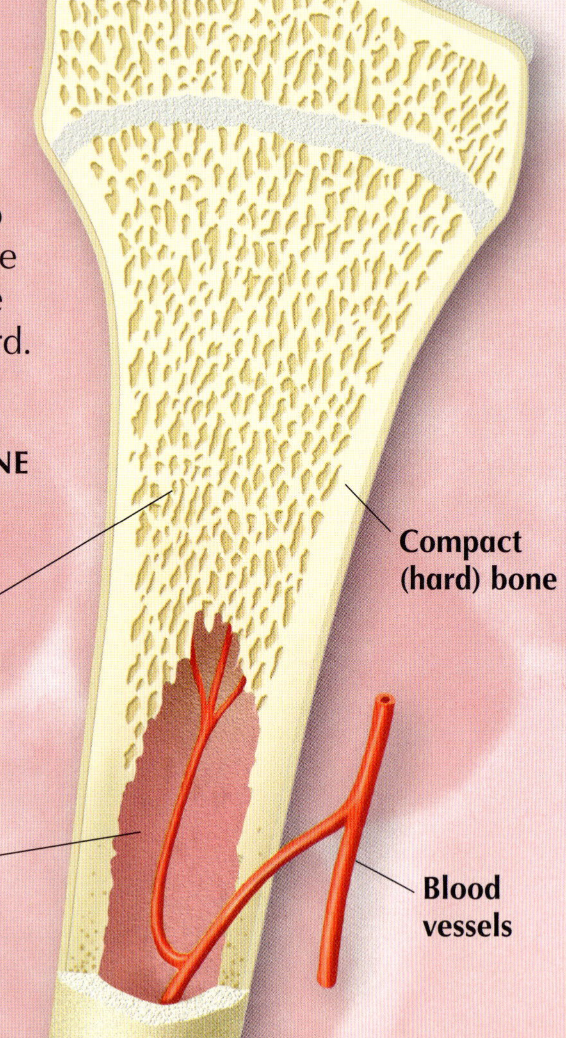

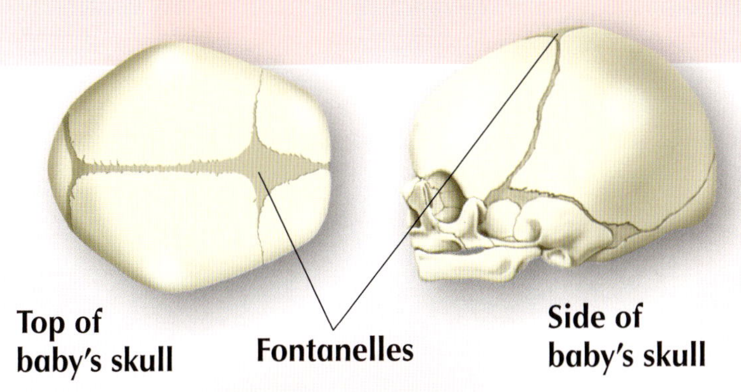

Holes in the head

A newborn baby's skull has slight gaps, called fontanelles, between some of its skull bones. These soft areas are squashed together during birth to help the baby's passage through the cervix.

Did you know?

- **A human skeleton made of steel would weigh five times more than a real skeleton of bones.**
- **If bones have to cope regularly with doing more work —for example, by lifting weights— they grow thicker and stronger.**
- **When we get older, we lose some of the minerals that make up our bones. This can make them brittle and they can break more easily than when we are younger.**

Inside the bone

The strands that make up the spongy bone are arranged so they can absorb the stresses and strains that we put on them as we go through our daily lives. In our longest bones, such as those in our legs, the spongy bone gives way to the medullary cavity, an opening that is full of bone marrow (see below).

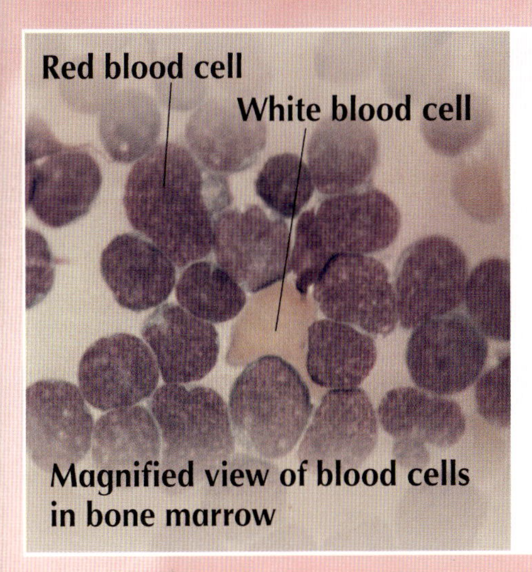

Magnified view of blood cells in bone marrow

Blood cells

The bone marrow makes new blood cells (see pages 52–53) to replace old cells that die. The blood cells all start out the same but then change as they develop to form red blood cells, white blood cells, and platelets.

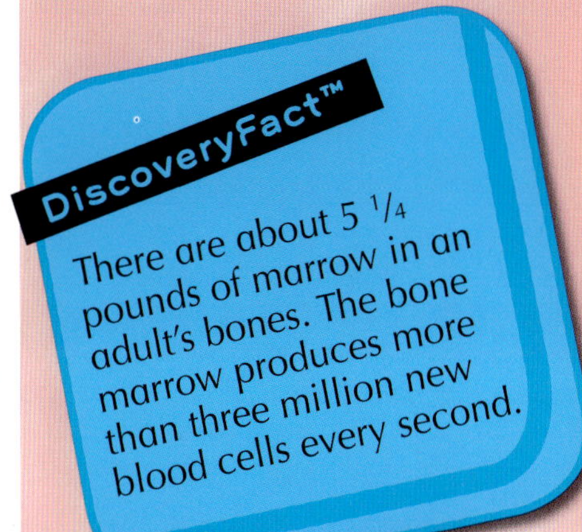

Joining bones

Your bones would fall apart if they were not fastened together by joints. Each joint lets your bones move in a certain direction and by a particular amount. All together, the joints allow your body to move into an amazing variety of positions.

On the move

Joints are classified by two methods: their structure and the movement they produce. A joint's structure depends upon many different things. These include whether the joint is stuck tightly together to form a suture (see page 25), or whether it contains cartilage to make the bone movement easier.

Types of joints

In some joints, the ball-shaped end of one bone fits into a bowl-shaped socket in the other bone. These ball-and-socket joints let the bones move to and fro and sideways and allow them to twist. They are found in the shoulder and hip. In hinge joints, the bones can move to and fro but not sideways. Hinge joints are found in the knees and the finger knuckles.

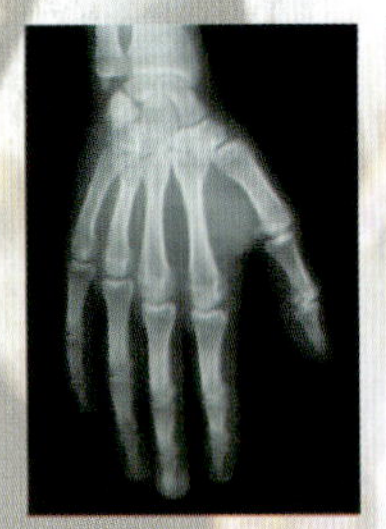

Gliding joints in the hand

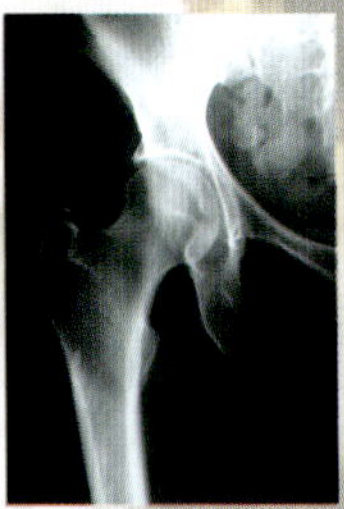

Ball-and-socket joint in the hip

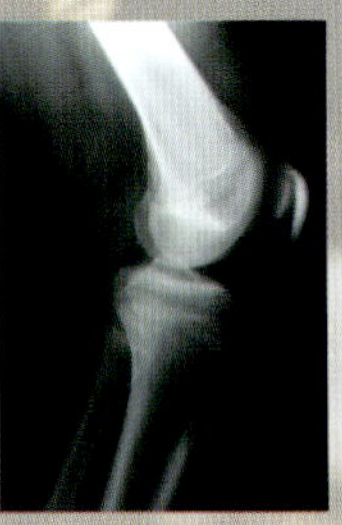

Hinge joint in the knee

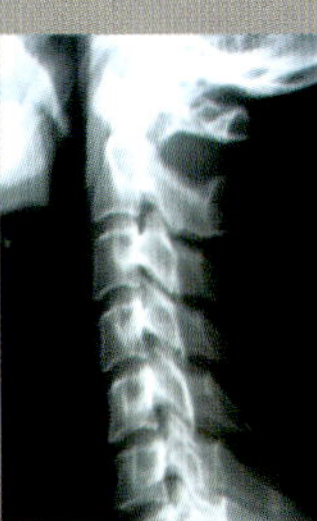

Many joints in the spine

Lots of joints

Some joints have more than two bones—for example, there are eight bones in the wrist and seven in the ankle. Each of these bones links to those next to it via a gliding joint, in which the bones slide and tilt against each other. The joints in the wrist are flexible, and they allow the hand to move in many positions. The joints in the ankle are less flexible but much stronger so that they can support the weight of the body.

Did you know?

- There are more than 350 joints in the body.
- The biggest joint is in the knee.
- The most flexible joint is in the shoulder.
- Some joints cannot move at all. These include the joints between the bones in the skull and the joints between the six bones in the hips.

DiscoveryFact™

The body's tiniest joint is on the smallest bone, the stirrup, which is deep inside the ear. The whole joint is smaller than this letter "o" here.

This gymnast's joints allow her body to move into many different positions.

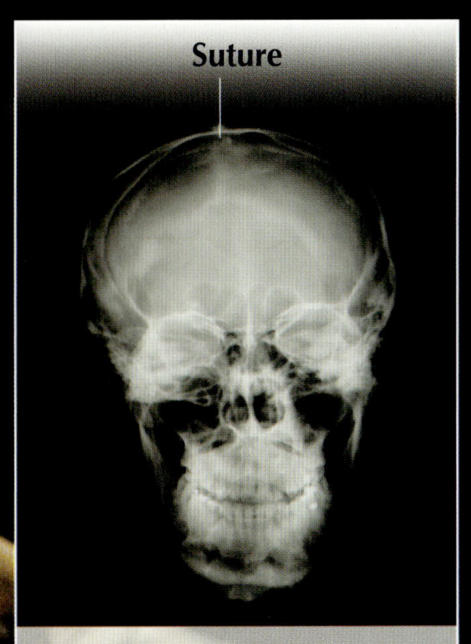

Skull joints

An adult's skull bones are joined together with strong fibers set into a kind of glue. These fixed, or immovable, joints look like wiggly lines and are known as sutures.

Ready to throw

Throwing a ball is a good example of how the joints all work together. Just before the ball is released, the joints of the hips, back, shoulder, elbow, wrist, and fingers all move in a fast sequence, one after the other, to hurl the ball at great speed.

A baseball pitcher "winds up" before releasing the ball.

Muscles

Almost half of the body is made of muscles. There are hundreds of them, and they power every movement we make. Muscles have to perform just one task—get shorter.

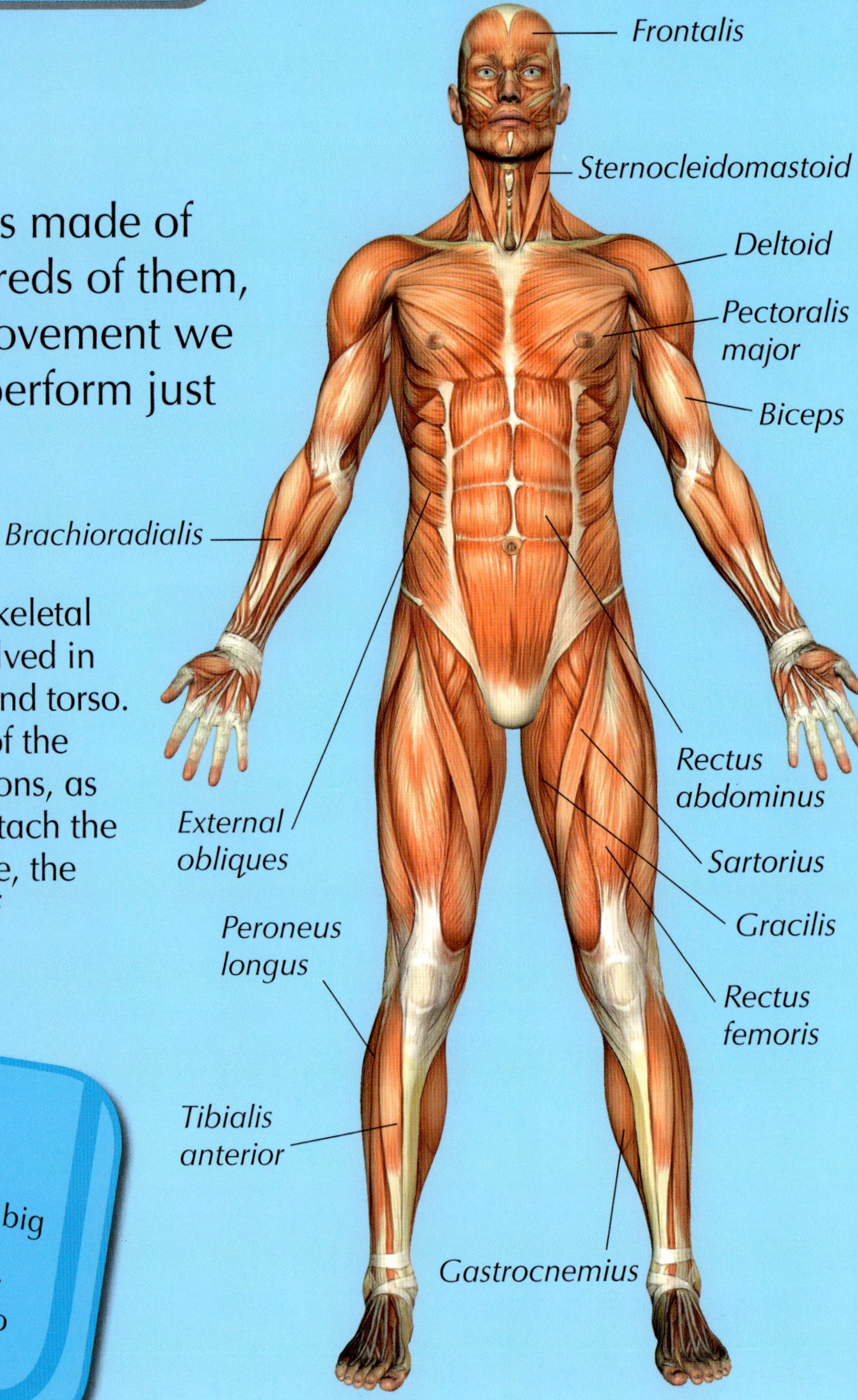

Skeletal muscles

Most of the body's muscles are skeletal muscles. These muscles are involved in moving our head, neck, limbs, and torso. They are attached to the bones of the skeleton by tough, ropelike tendons, as opposed to the ligaments that attach the bones to each other. For example, the Achilles tendon attaches the calf muscle to the heel.

DiscoveryFact™

The smallest muscle is not even as big as this "i." It is called the stapedius and is inside the ear. It pulls the ear bones to stop them from shaking too much during very loud noises.

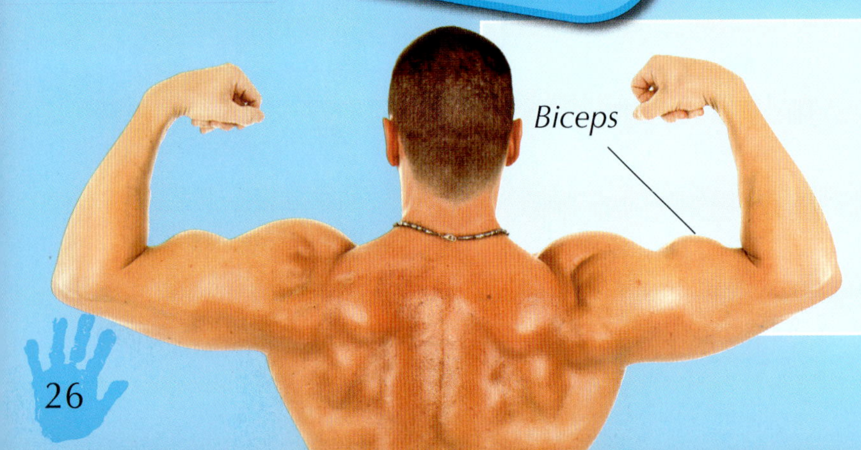

More muscles?

Bodybuilders who exercise to build up their muscles don't have more muscles than anyone else. Each muscle just becomes bigger and bulges more under the skin.

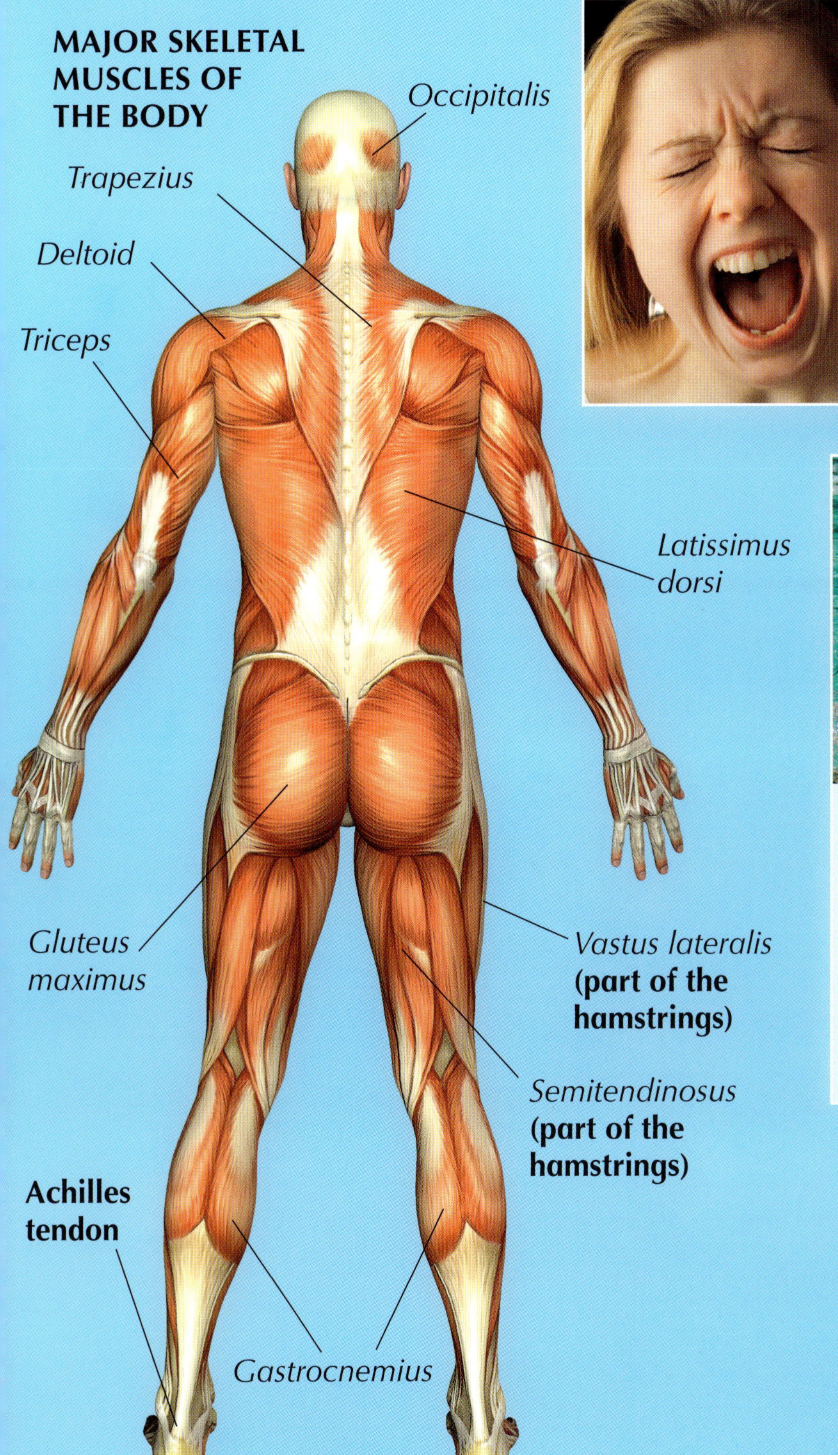

Noise muscles

Your skeletal muscles are also involved in some small, less obvious actions. For example, when you talk or shout, the breathing muscles push out air from the lungs and through the voice box.

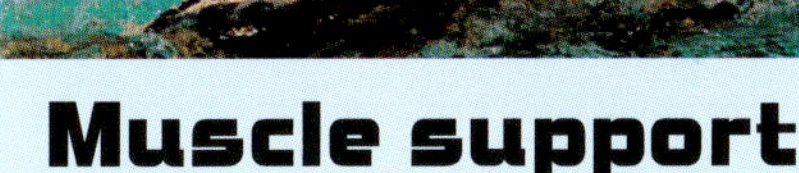

Muscle support

Swimming is especially good for the muscles and joints. It exercises muscles that are rarely used, and the water supports the body so the joints do not get injured.

Muscle names

Some of the body's muscles have scientific names, and a few of these have become well known. The *pectoralis major* muscles, or pectorals, are in the upper chest. The *rectus abdominus* muscles, or abdominals, are in the front of the abdomen. The biceps is the bulging muscle in the upper arm. The hamstrings are the common name given to the strong muscles at the rear of the thigh.

Did you know?

- **The body has about 650 muscles.**
- **The biggest muscle is the** *gluteus maximus* **in the buttock.**
- **The longest muscle is the** *sartorius* **muscle. It runs down the front of the upper leg.**

Making faces

Did you know that we can communicate without saying a single word! The muscles in our faces can make a lot of small or large movements, pulling parts of the face and allowing us to show a vast range of feelings, moods, and emotions.

Expressions

The face has more than 60 muscles. We use them all the time, often without realizing it. As people look at us, our faces show what we are thinking and feeling. We can try to control our facial expressions for a time, but it's hard to fake them for long. Actors learn to control their facial expressions when they pretend to have certain feelings and emotions.

MAJOR MUSCLES OF THE FACE

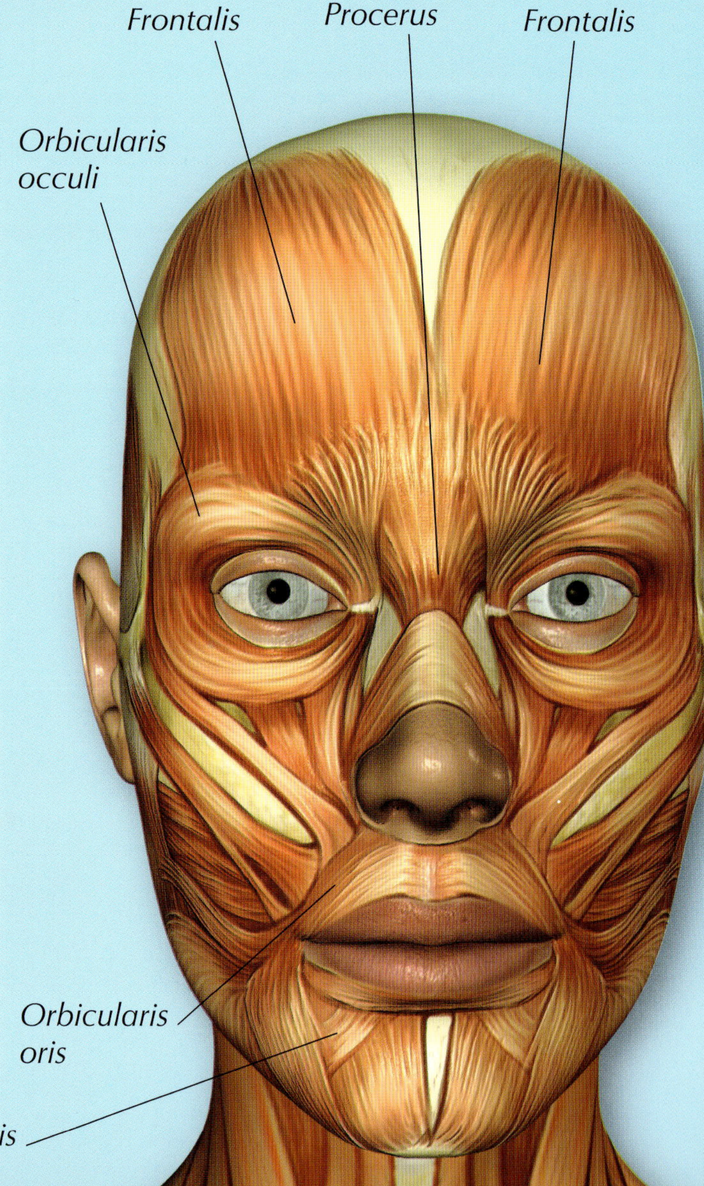

Making faces

The facial muscles are at different angles to each other. They can pull the skin, lips, cheeks, and other features into a great many positions. For example, the eyebrows are raised by contracting the *frontalis* muscle that runs vertically along the forehead. This muscle is also used when we frown.

A girl uses her face muscles to create a funny face.

Facial emotions

- Look in a mirror and watch your eyebrows closely.
- Raise them high and you look surprised.
- Lower them slightly and you look puzzled.
- Lower them more and you look annoyed.
- Now, bring them really low and you look very angry.

"Smiling" chimp

Many animals, such as chimps, seem to smile, but we must be careful not to assume that their expressions are the same as ours. In fact, a chimp bares its teeth, or "smiles," when it is afraid and ready to defend itself.

A chimp "smiles" to show fear.

Facial muscles

Most muscles are joined to bones, but in the face the muscles are joined to each other or to the skin. They contract by tiny amounts, making other muscles nearby stretch. When the muscles do this, they move the skin and make the facial features, such as the eyebrows and lips, move. All of this produces a facial expression.

The major muscles of the side of the head with their scientific names

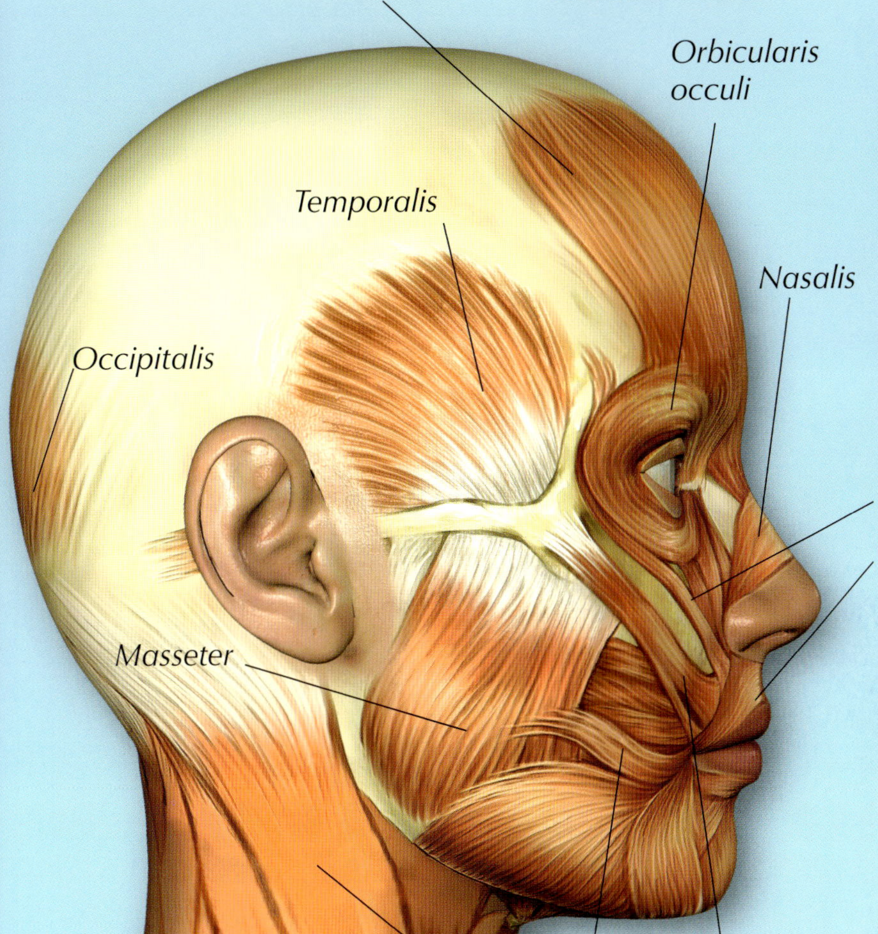

DiscoveryFact™

It's easier to smile than to frown! A happy smile uses less than 20 face muscles. A sad frown needs twice as many. Save energy and smile!

Quick Quiz

Are these sentences TRUE or FALSE? Place the correct sticker in the box.

1. [ ] The human skeleton has a total of 565 bones.
2. [ ] A newborn baby's skull has a slight gap.
3. [ ] The body's tiniest joint is inside the knee.
4. [ ] The biggest muscle is the *gluteus maximus* in the buttock.
5. [ ] The face has more than 150 muscles.

Find the stickers to finish the diagram.

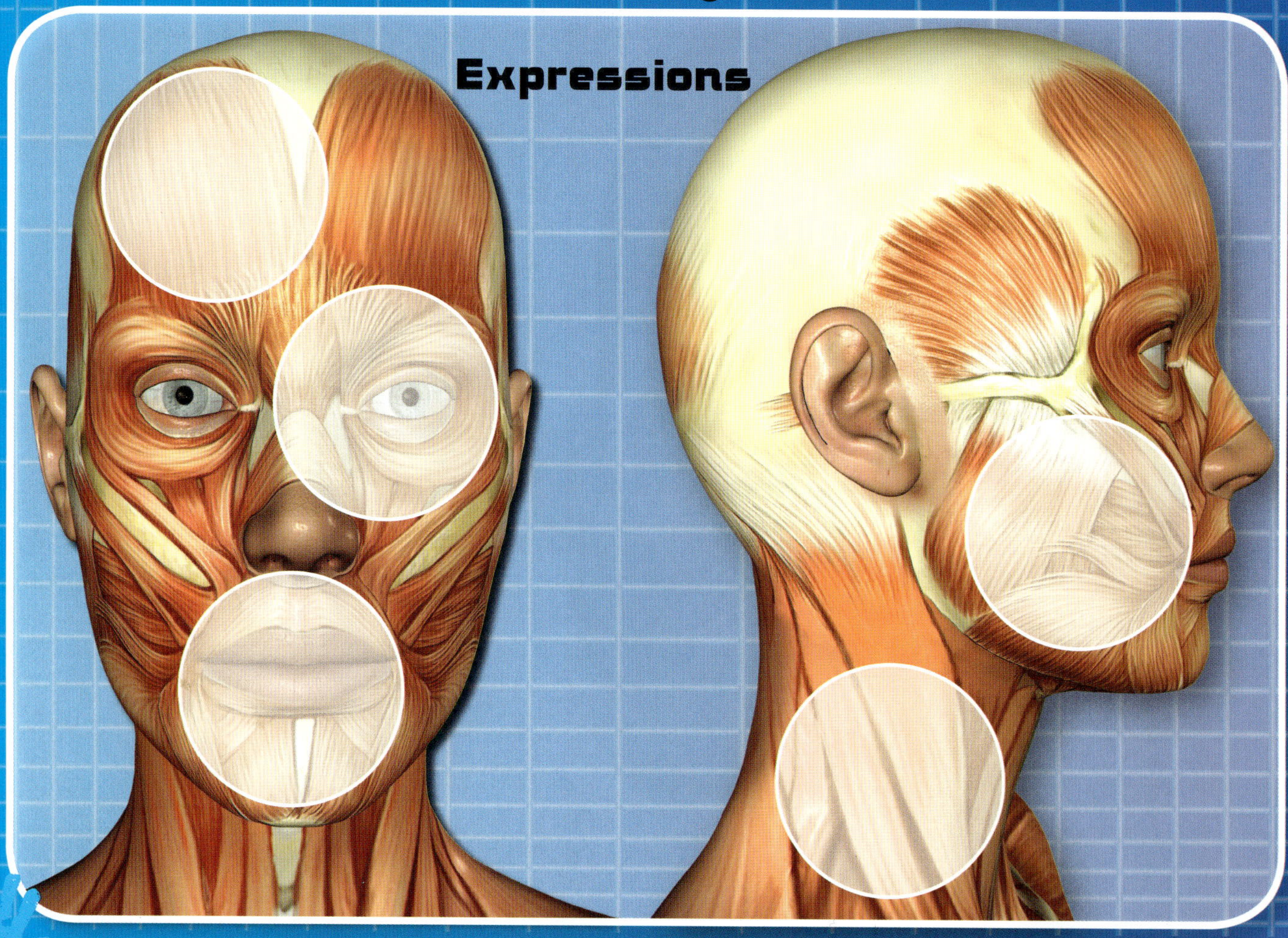

ANSWERS: 1 – F, 2 – T, 3 – F, 4 – T, 5 – F

Lungs and breathing

In an emergency, your body can make do without food for several days, and it can even cope without water for a day or so. But one thing is so vital that your body cannot survive more than a few minutes without it—oxygen. You take in oxygen from the air around you by breathing, using the parts of the body called the respiratory system. You don't have to think about breathing—your body does it automatically—but it keeps you alive.

Breathing system

The respiratory, or breathing, system is located in the head, neck, and chest. You use it to draw air deep into your lungs. Here, oxygen passes into the blood and then spreads all around your body.

Bigger and smaller

The lungs act like two balloons inside your chest. As you draw air into the breathing system the lungs get bigger as they fill with air. Then when you breathe out, air is pushed out of the lungs and they get smaller.

MAIN PARTS OF THE RESPIRATORY SYSTEM

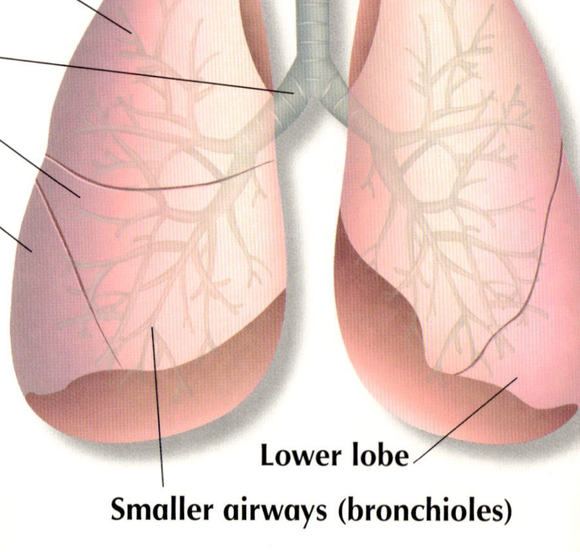

The airways

The upper airways in the head and neck include the throat and the nasal chamber (see page 36). The lower airways include the windpipe in the neck and the tubes called bronchi and bronchioles, which carry air into the lungs. At the top of the windpipe is the larynx, or voice box, which produces the voice when air passes through it.

Fanning the flames

In ancient times, many people thought that body warmth came from food being burned in the heart. They believed that breathing was a way of providing air for the burning flames in the heart. They thought that when the body was active, breathing increased to provide more air to fan the flames, making the body hotter.

Down into the lungs

The breathing muscles create the movement that sucks air in and pushes air out of your lungs. The most important muscles are the dome-shaped diaphragm below the lungs and the long muscles between the ribs called intercostals. The backbone, ribs, and breastbone form a cage around the lungs, which protects these parts yet still allows the breathing action (see pages 42–43).

DiscoveryFact™

A free diver is someone who dives underwater without an air tank. Some free divers can hold their breath for more than six minutes when they dive.

Sense of smell

Air coming in through the nose carries tiny particles of smell chemicals. These particles land on sensitive patches in the roof of the nasal chamber. The patches work out the type of particle and send information about the smell to the brain (see pages 88–89).

Blowing

In normal breathing, air flows in and out through the nose, but the air flow can be directed out through the mouth. This is useful for all kinds of actions, from blowing out candles to playing the trumpet.

The nose

Most air is breathed in through the nose. Inside the nose, air is cleaned, warmed, and moistened to make it more suitable for traveling into the lungs. Dusty, cold, or dry air can clog the lungs or dry out the airways.

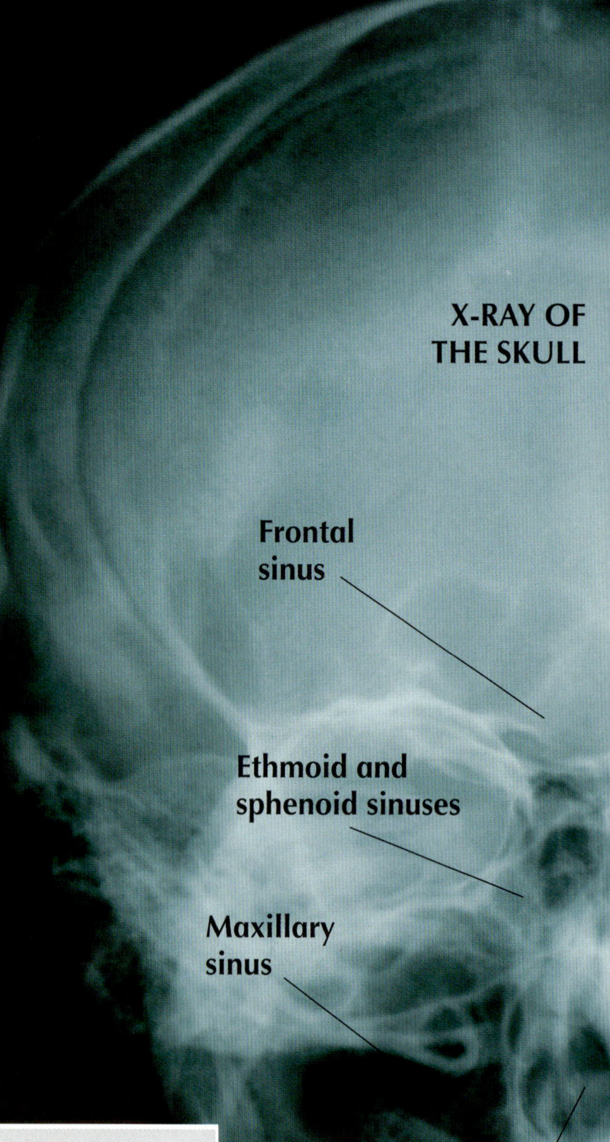

Air filters

The nose is separated into two nostrils by a wall of cartilage. The nostrils have small hairs inside them that catch bits of dust and other particles floating in the air. The nostrils are the entrance to the nasal cavity, an air-filled space that works like an air filter. The lining of the nasal cavity is coated with a layer of mucus, a thick, sticky fluid that moistens the air and traps germs, dust, and other particles.

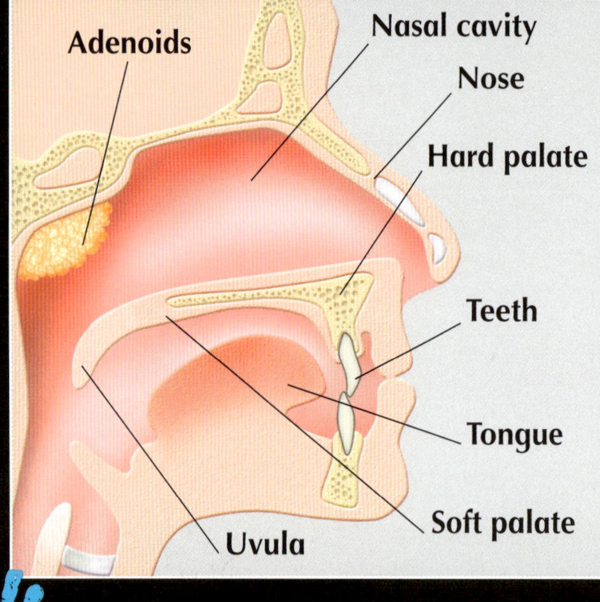

Nasal cavity

The nasal cavity is separated from the mouth by the palate, which is divided into the hard, bony palate at the front and the soft palate at the back. The adenoids are bulges of tissue that help to trap and remove germs from air.

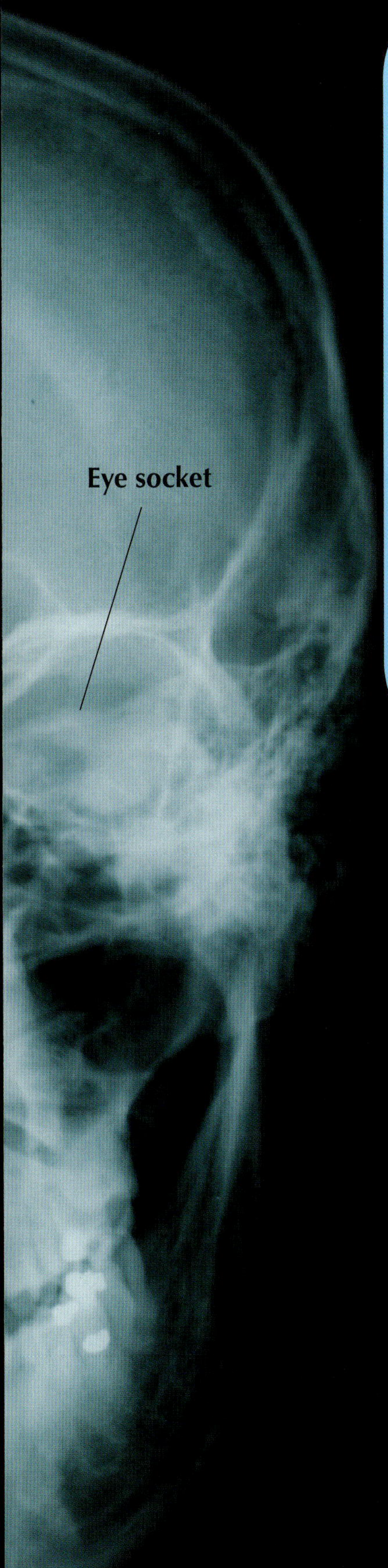

Did you know?

- Branching off the nasal cavity are a number of air-filled spaces called sinuses.
- There are four sets of sinuses in the skull. These are the frontal, ethmoid, sphenoid, and maxillary sinuses.
- No one knows exactly what the sinuses are for, but they may be used to help to make the different sounds of speech, or to help with temperature control within the head, or to make the bones of the skull lighter.

Synchronized swimmers

Closed nose

Synchronized swimmers usually wear a nose clip when they are performing. This stops water from entering the nasal cavity and irritating the cavity lining, especially when the swimmers are upside down in the pool.

Warmed by blood

The nasal cavity has a thin lining with a network of blood vessels just beneath the surface. The warm blood flowing through these vessels gives out heat to the passing air. These blood vessels are delicate—a bang to the nose may break one and cause a nosebleed.

Face masks

People with certain jobs, such as builders and miners, wear masks with filters. These masks stop dust particles, which the nasal cavity cannot trap, from entering the breathing system, where they might cause damage.

Dust mask

In the throat

The throat has two functions: it is a passageway for air and food. Swallowing closes off the windpipe, so food is not accidentally carried into the lower airways.

The right way

When you swallow, the entrance to the windpipe tilts up and forward and a stiff flap—the epiglottis—tilts down over it. This piece of cartilage blocks the upper entrance to your windpipe, which means that food slides down into the esophagus. It is not possible to breathe when swallowing because the windpipe is closed.

When we eat, as these women are, we do not usually think about the action of swallowing—we just do it.

Nasal cavity
Pharynx
Larynx
Spinal cord
Mouth
Uvula
Epiglottis
Esophagus
Trachea

Open wide

The throat connects your mouth and nasal cavity to your trachea, or windpipe, and the esophagus, which is a tube down to the stomach. The upper part of the throat is called the pharynx. Below this is the larynx, or voice box, which is the opening to the respiratory tract. At the sides of the throat there are bulges of special germ-killing tissue called the tonsils, which, like the adenoids, help to fight infection.

Swollen tonsils

The tonsils may swell when they are fighting germs in the body, causing a sore throat and discomfort when swallowing. This illness is called tonsillitis.

A child with swollen tonsils

The wrong way

Very rarely, swallowed food may go down "the wrong way." This means it goes into the windpipe and blocks the airway. If this happens, breathing becomes difficult and can even stop, causing choking. Usually a cough removes the blockage by forcing fast-moving air up from the lungs. This blows the food up into the throat for safe swallowing.

Choking

If coughing cannot remove an obstruction from the windpipe, a trained person may have to perform the Heimlich maneuver. This is done by quickly squeezing the lower chest to press the lungs, which forces air and the blockage out.

Voice box

The larynx, or voice box, is at the top of the trachea, or windpipe. In men and some women, it can be seen as a hard bulge at the front of the neck, which is called the Adam's apple. The larynx allows us to make vocalizations, or sounds, that can range from a quiet whisper to a loud shout.

This opera singer has learned how to control her vocal cords to produce beautiful sounds.

Vocal cords

Two flaplike strips, or ridges, stick out from the inside of your voice box (see below). These are your vocal cords. In normal breathing, the vocal cords are held apart by muscles. This forms a V-shaped gap between them, which is known as the glottis. Air passes silently through the glottis when you are breathing normally.

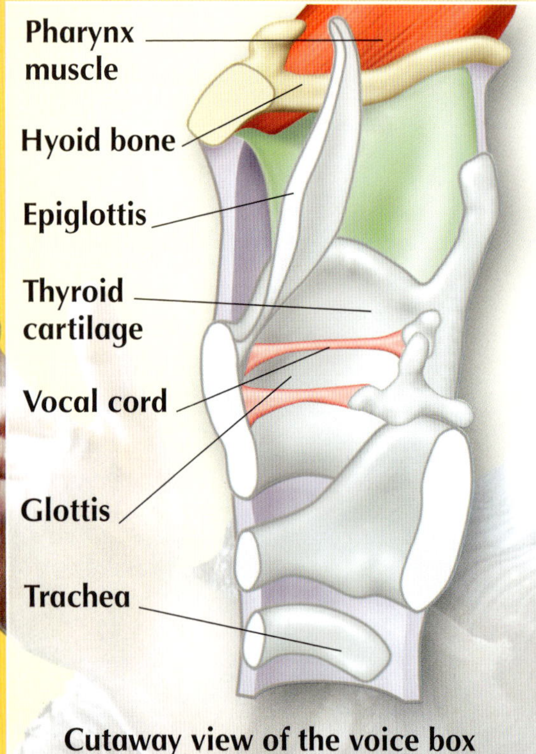

Cutaway view of the voice box

Voice box

The voice box is made of nine curved plates of cartilage. The main cartilage plate is the thyroid cartilage. These plates help to keep the voice box open. There are also muscles connected to the cartilage plates, which move the plates to change the shape of the vocal cords and the size of the glottis.

Did you know?

- Women's voices are usually higher than men's because their vocal cords are shorter and vibrate more quickly.
- Men's vocal cords are $^{2}/_{3}$–1 inch long, while women's vocal cords are $^{1}/_{2}$–$^{2}/_{3}$ inch in length.

Vocal sounds

The wide range of sounds you can make with your voice is controlled by the vibration of the vocal cords. When the muscles pull on your vocal cords, they make the gap between the cords narrower. Air flowing from the lungs through this narrow gap makes the cords vibrate, or shake fast. This produces the basic sounds of the voice. The sounds are altered and made louder by the air spaces in the mouth, the nose, and the sinuses. The shapes of these spaces vary from person to person, which is why each of us has a unique and individual voice.

A teacher introduces some of the different sounds required to speak French.

Pronunciation

You use your tongue, cheeks, and mouth to speak the words you use every day. When you learn a new language, you may have to learn how to make completely new sounds. To do this, you will have to create new shapes with your mouth, cheeks, teeth, and tongue so that you can pronounce foreign words correctly.

Speaking while breathing

- The vocal cords only work properly with air that is being breathed out.
- Test this by speaking while breathing in. It's much harder than speaking normally, and the sounds seem to disappear into your chest.

The lungs

The lungs are like elastic bags filled
with millions of tiny balloons. In
each lung, the branching airways
become thinner and shorter
until, finally, they are narrower
than human hairs.

Lungs and lobes

Each lung is made up of sections called lobes, and each lobe has a bronchus leading to it. The right lung has three lobes—upper, middle, and lower. The left lung is smaller and has only two lobes—upper and lower—because it has a scooped-out area where the heart sits. The esophagus and the main blood vessels lie between the lungs.

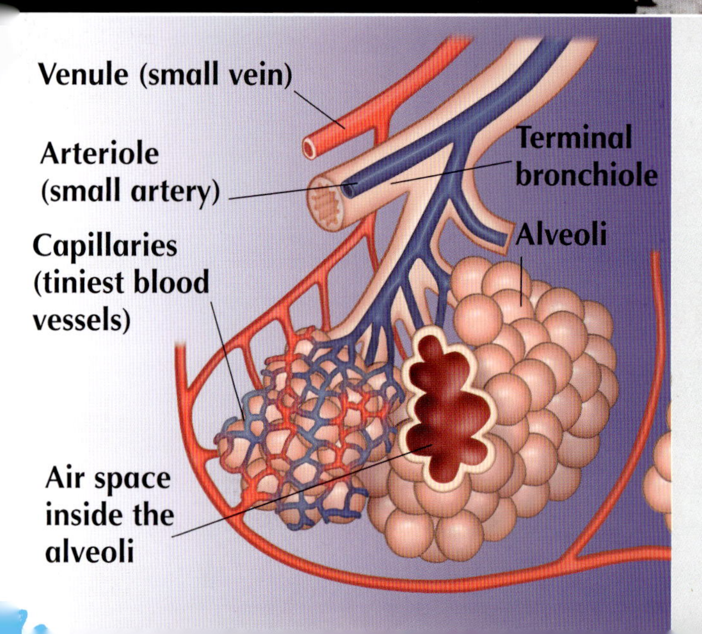

Into the blood

The smallest airways, called the terminal bronchioles, carry air to groups of microscopic, bubble-shaped air sacs called alveoli. The alveoli are surrounded by lots of blood vessels so that oxygen can pass easily from the lungs and into the blood.

A resin cast showing the smaller and smaller airways inside the lungs

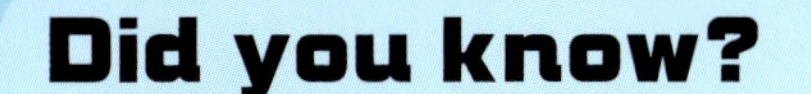

Did you know?

- Each lung has about 300 million alveoli.
- Each alveolus is about $^{1}/_{125}$ inch in diameter.
- The name alveolus comes from the Latin word meaning "little cavity."
- If spread out, the millions of alveoli in a pair of lungs would cover the area of a tennis court.

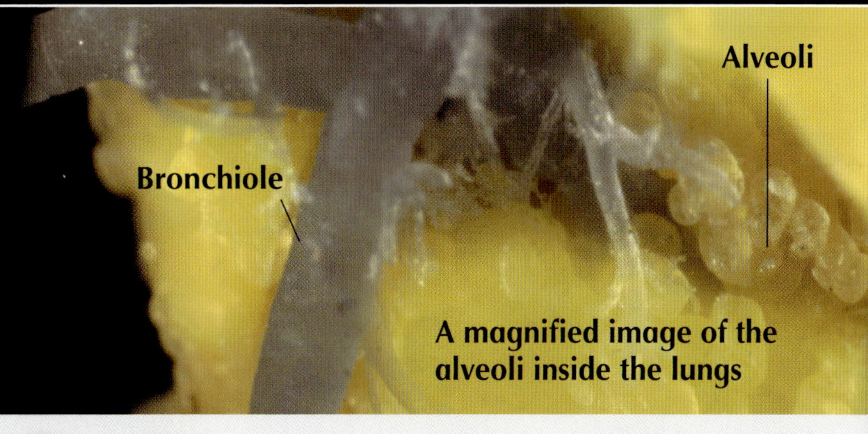

A magnified image of the alveoli inside the lungs

Alveoli

Under a microscope, alveoli look like small, almost see-through balloons. Most alveoli are not separate from each other but are squashed together so that they look like bunches of grapes. As a result of this, they are partly merged inside and have one large, shared air space.

Into the blood

Oxygen from inhaled air passes into the body through the alveoli. It seeps from the air in the alveoli into the blood in the microscopic blood vessels, known as capillaries, around the alveoli. This is also where the waste gas carbon dioxide moves from the blood into the alveoli and is eventually exhaled.

DiscoveryFact™

The lungs are the only part of the body that could float on water. In fact, people float more easily on water if they breathe in deeply, and then take small breaths, keeping the lungs as full of air as possible.

Breathing

The actions of the main breathing muscles—the intercostals and the diaphragm—are performed automatically. As a result, you do not usually have to think about breathing in and out.

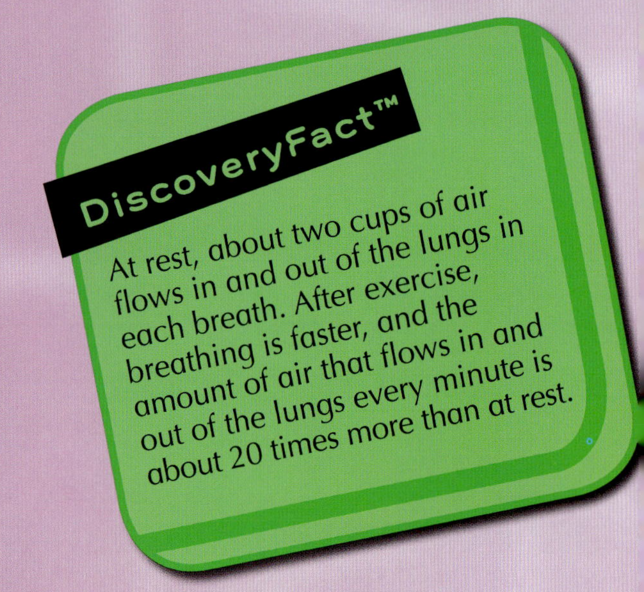

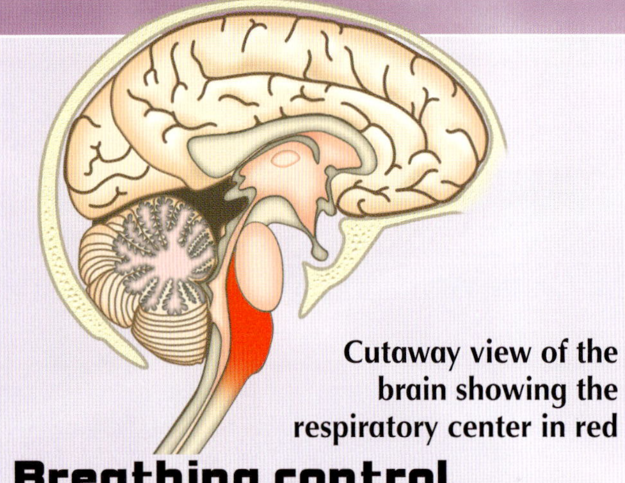

Cutaway view of the brain showing the respiratory center in red

Breathing control

The breathing muscles are controlled by signals from a part of the brain called the respiratory center. This detects the amounts of oxygen and carbon dioxide in the blood. As carbon dioxide levels rise and oxygen levels fall, the brain tells the breathing muscles to work harder.

Breathing in

To inhale, or breathe in, the diaphragm contracts, becoming flatter. This pulls the lungs downward. At the same time, the intercostal muscles contract and make the ribs move up and out. The result is that the lungs are stretched and suck air in through the nose and down the windpipe into the chest.

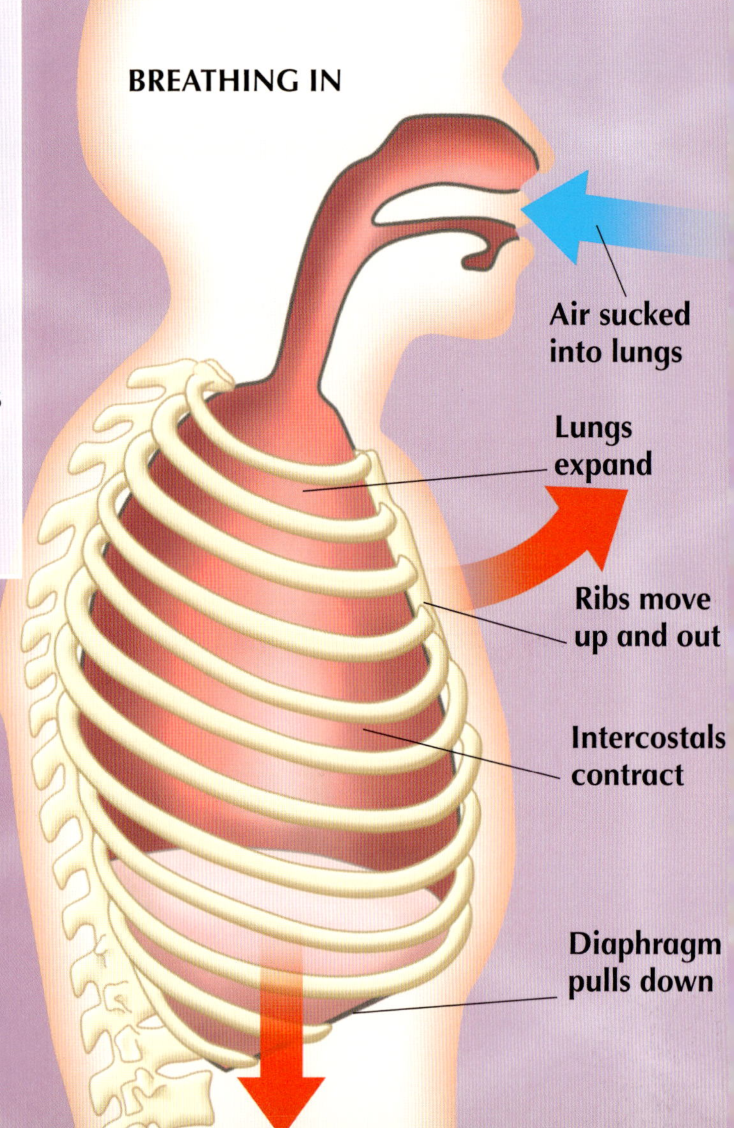

Breathing rate

- Rest for a few minutes, then count how many breaths you take in one minute. Next, jog on the spot for three minutes, then count your breaths.
- Rest again, then count your breaths again. Your breathing rate should rise after activity, then gradually return to its resting rate.

A boy holds his breath while jumping into water.

Stop breathing

We have to make ourselves stop breathing when we jump into water. The brain tries to make us breathe, but we can prevent it for a while so that our lungs do not fill with water.

Breathing out

To exhale, or breathe out, the diaphragm and the intercostals all relax. The lungs, which have stretched like a rubber band, spring back to their usual shape. This makes the diaphragm return to its dome shape and the ribs move down and in. As the lungs shrink, they push air up the windpipe and out through the nose.

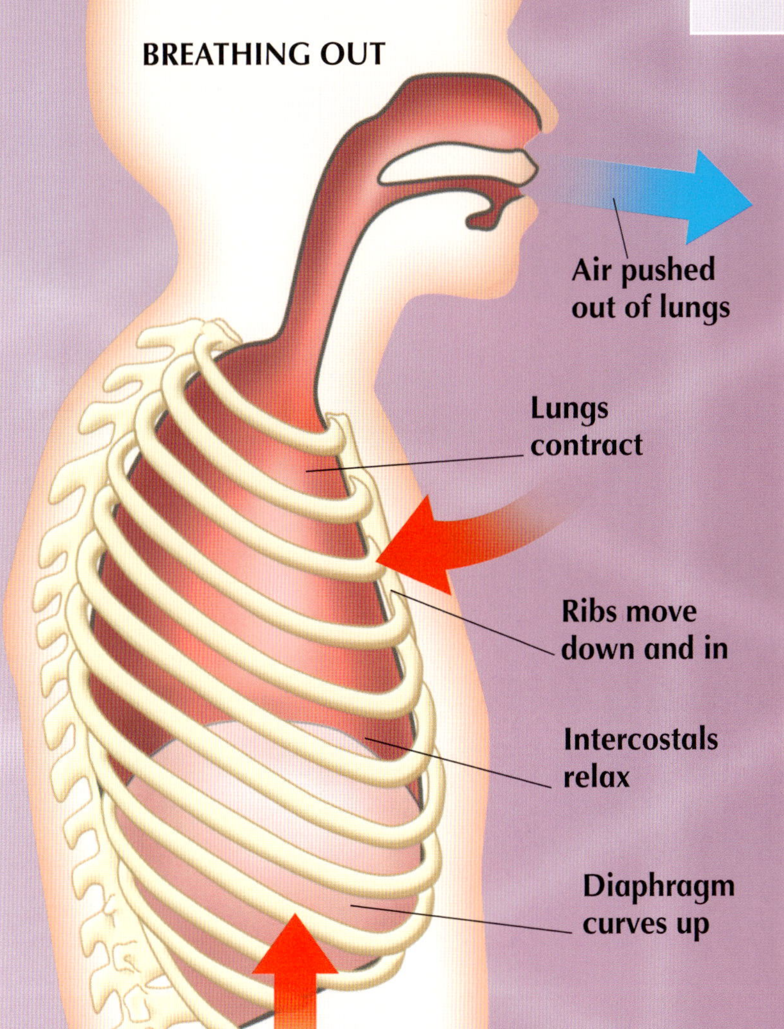

Mouth-to-mouth

Exhaled air still contains some oxygen. It can be blown into someone's lungs in an emergency if he or she has stopped breathing. This is called artificial respiration.

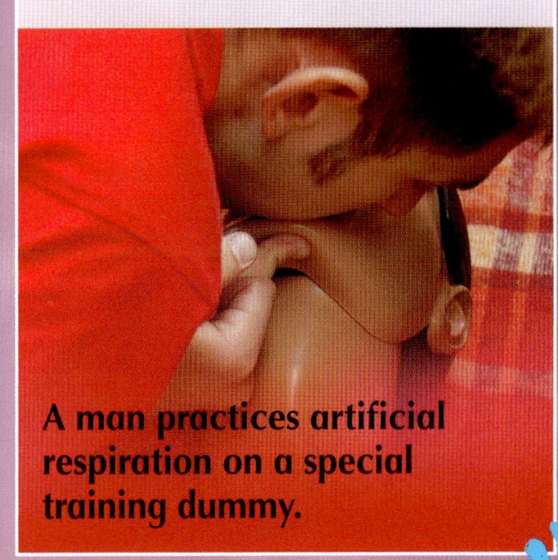

A man practices artificial respiration on a special training dummy.

Quick Quiz

Are these sentences TRUE or FALSE?
Place the correct sticker in the box.

1. Body warmth comes from food burning in the heart.
2. There are four sets of sinuses in the skull.
3. Women's voices are higher than men's because their vocal cords are shorter.
4. Each lung has 30 alveoli.
5. The heart is the only part of the body that can float on water.

Find the stickers to finish the diagrams.

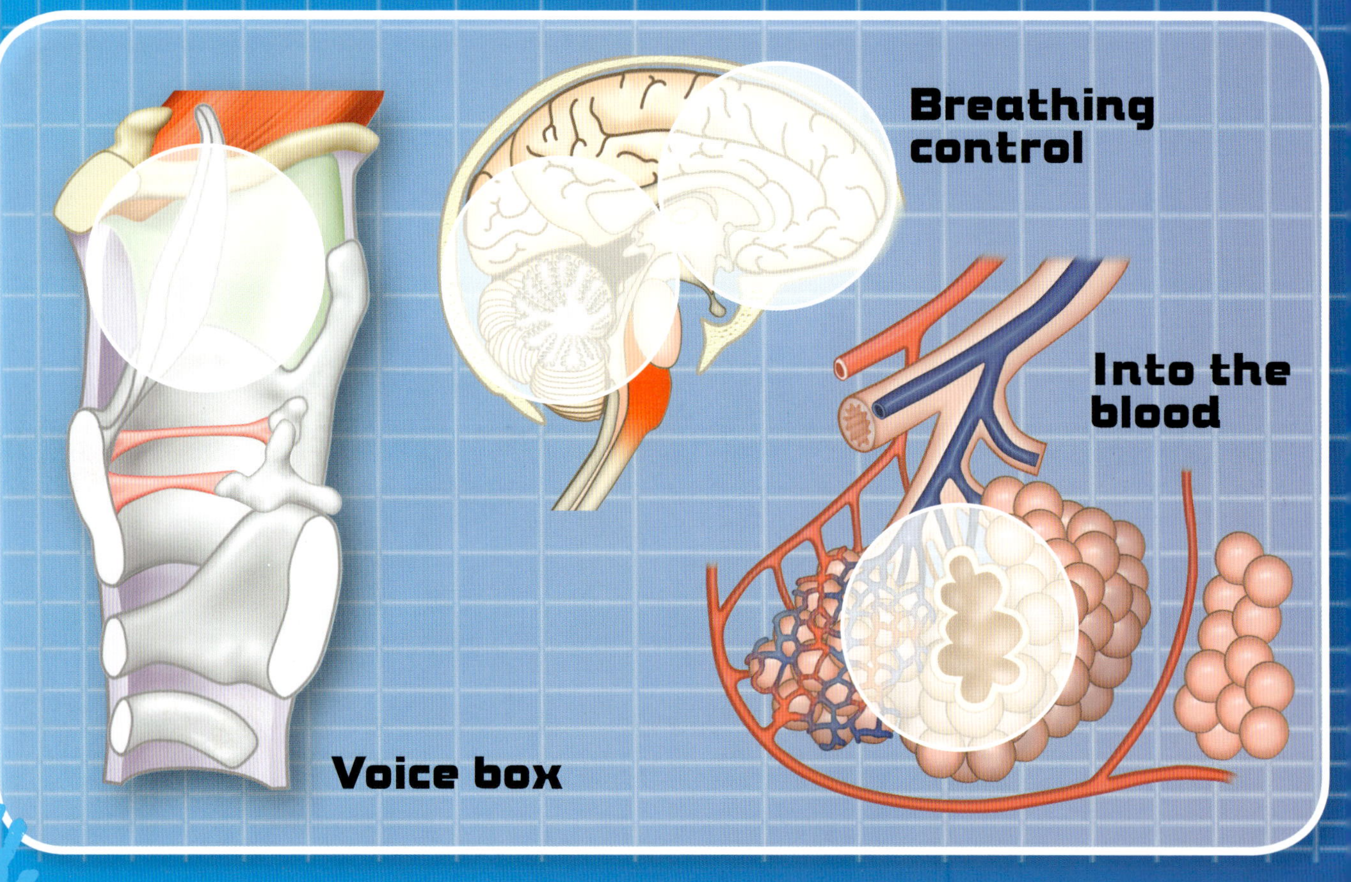

ANSWERS: 1 – F, 2 – T, 3 – T, 4 – F, 5 – F

Heart and blood

The heart is an amazing pump that works nonstop, keeping the body alive. With every beat, it sends a surge of bright red blood, carrying vital supplies, such as oxygen, and the body's waste products, such as carbon dioxide, through a network of blood vessels to and from every part of the body. The heart, blood, and vessels are together known as the circulatory, or cardiovascular, system.

The pump

The heart is a muscular pump that works constantly to squeeze blood into blood vessels called arteries. The arteries take the blood around the body, and the veins return the blood to the heart.

The mechanical pump of a fountain uses force to squirt water a great distance.

Powerful pump

Just as a fountain forces water out, the heart muscle contracts to push blood at great force into the arteries. Your heart will do this about two-and-a-half billion times during your life.

The right pump

The heart is really two pumps side by side. The right pump sends blood along the pulmonary arteries to the lungs, where it absorbs oxygen. This blood then comes back through the pulmonary veins to the left side of the heart to be pumped around the rest of the body (see right).

OUTSIDE VIEW OF THE HEART AND MAIN BLOOD VESSELS

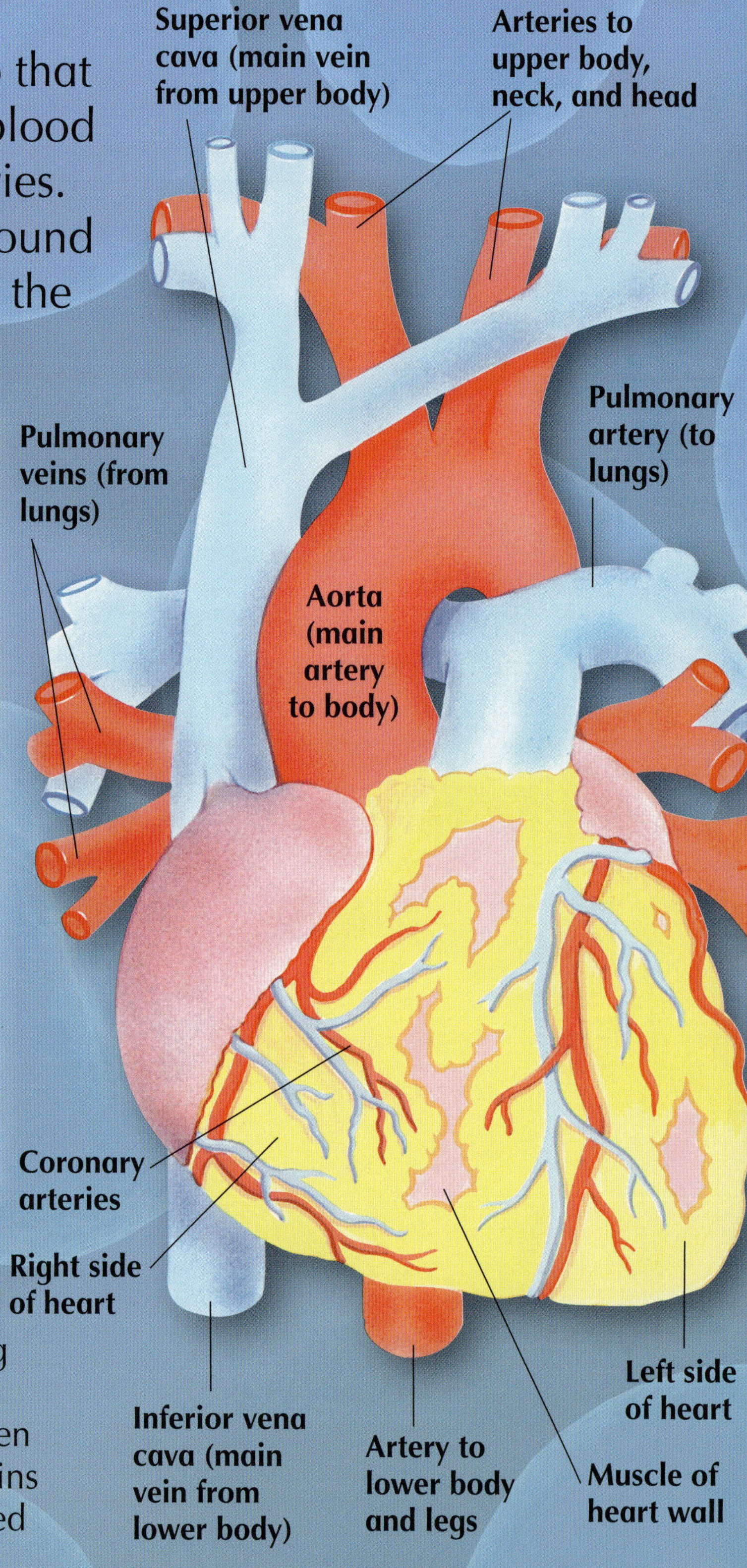

Valves stop blood from flowing the wrong way in the veins.

Valves

Normal direction of blood flow

Studying veins

The veins are just under the skin in some places, and can be seen as dark lines. The blood in the veins does not flow with as much pressure as the blood being forced through the arteries by the heart. Because vein blood flows with a lower pressure, there is a risk that it could flow the wrong way. To stop this, the larger veins have valves in them, and these slam shut to stop blood from flowing the wrong way.

DiscoveryFact™

With each pump, blood surges out into the main arteries at a speed of 16 inches per second. If it were to pass through a hole the size of a pinhead at this speed and pressure, it would spurt more than 10 feet.

The left pump

The left side of the heart is larger and more powerful than the right side. While the right side of the heart pumps blood to the lungs, the left side pumps blood all around the body, delivering oxygen, energy, and nutrients from food to every part. Then the blood, which is now low in oxygen, returns from all of these body parts through the veins to the heart's right side. There, it begins its nonstop journey back to the lungs and then around the body once again.

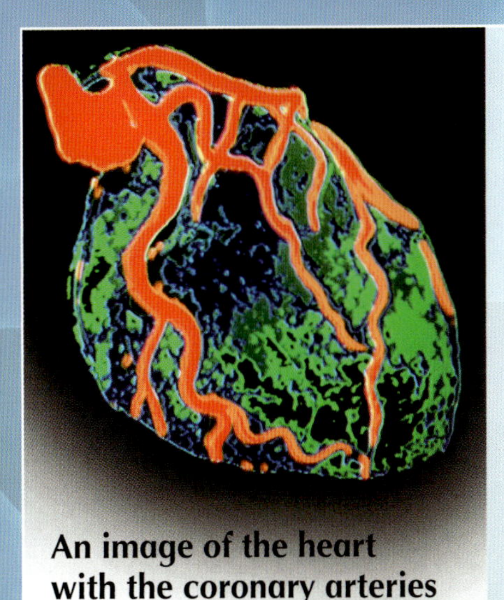

An image of the heart with the coronary arteries shown in red.

Blood supply

The heart muscle has its own blood supply—the coronary arteries. Blood flows through these arteries into the heart muscle and then out through the coronary veins. If the coronary arteries become blocked, the heart muscle may die. This is one form of a heart attack.

Harvey's discovery

For centuries, people believed that blood flowed into the body, where it was used up. In 1628, English physician William Harvey did experiments that showed that blood circulates around and around the body in the blood vessels, returning to the heart at the end of each circuit.

The heart

The heart is not a solid lump of muscle but it has four inner compartments, called chambers. Blood flows through these chambers, with four valves, or flaps, making sure that it flows the right way.

The arrows show the passage of blood from the body into the right side of the heart, then the passage of blood from the lungs through the left side of the heart.

Upper chambers

Each half of the heart has an upper chamber, which is called an atrium. The left atrium receives blood from the lungs. The right atrium takes in blood from the body.

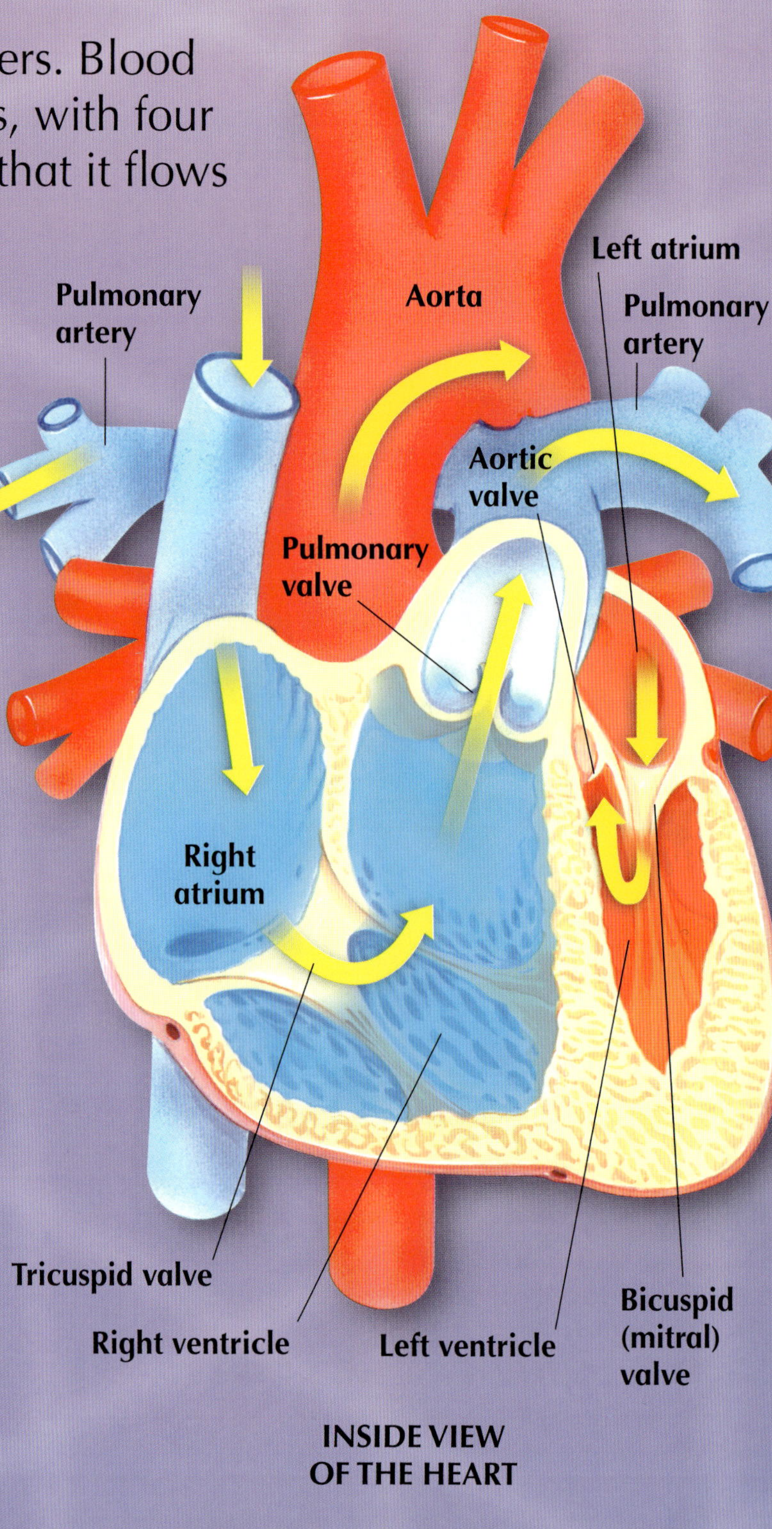

INSIDE VIEW OF THE HEART

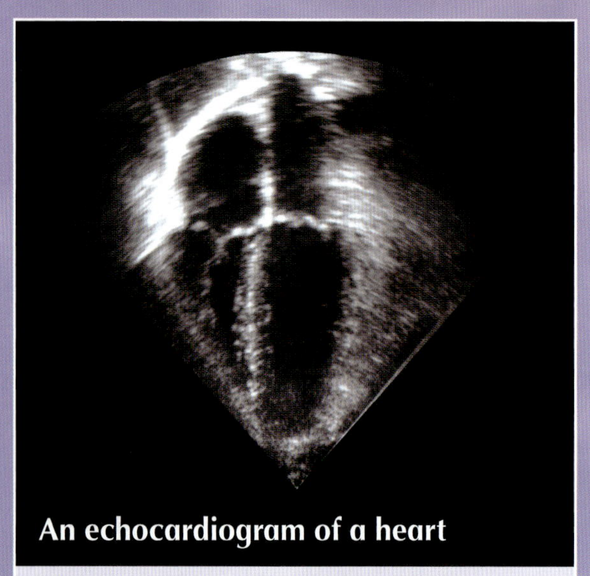

An echocardiogram of a heart

Echocardiogram

Sound waves can be beamed into the heart, where they hit different parts and echo back. These echoes form a moving picture called an echocardiogram, which shows the four chambers of the heart.

DiscoveryFact™

During a typical day, the adult heart pumps out about 2,000 gallons of blood. That would be enough blood to fill more than 50 bathtubs.

Lower chambers

Each side of the heart also has a lower chamber, which is called a ventricle. Each ventricle receives blood from the atrium above it through a funnel-shaped valve. As the ventricles squeeze, they push blood out through one-way valves into the main arteries.

Did you know?

- **In a typical adult at rest, the heart pumps about 70 times each minute and sends out about 1/3 cup of blood with each beat.**
- **The heart pumps about 5 quarts of blood each minute, which is the total volume of blood in an adult body. When the heart pumps faster, it sends out four times this amount.**

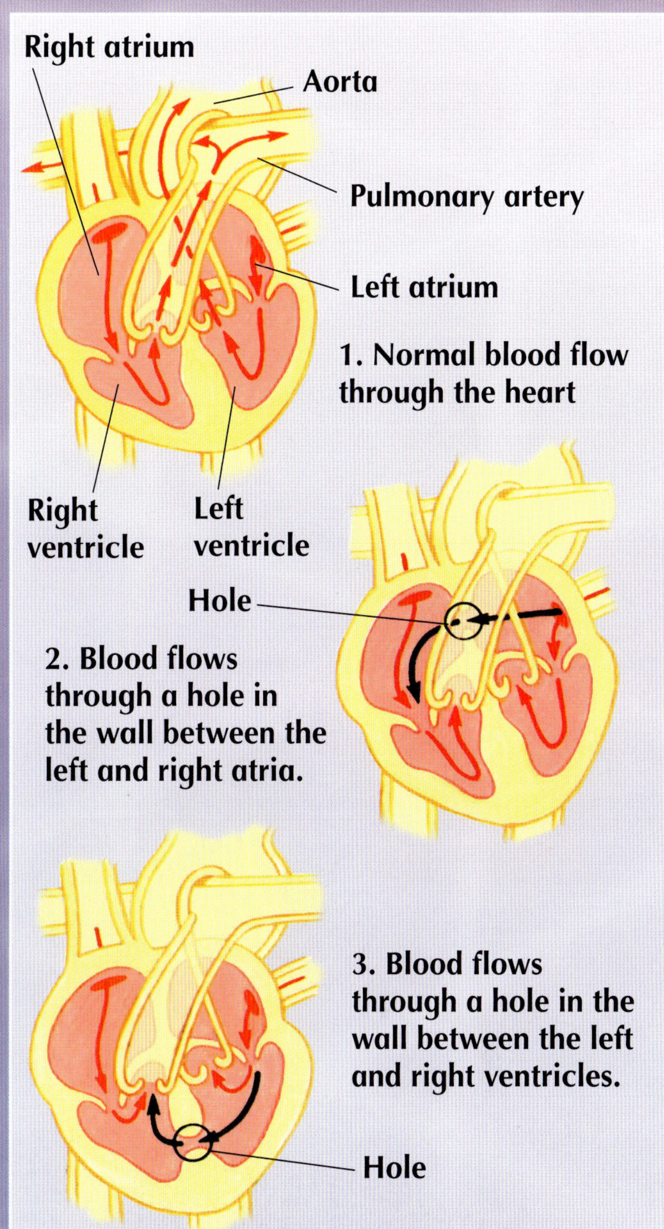

1. Normal blood flow through the heart

2. Blood flows through a hole in the wall between the left and right atria.

3. Blood flows through a hole in the wall between the left and right ventricles.

Hole in the heart

Some babies are born with a heart problem called a "hole in the heart." With this condition, blood from one side of the heart can mix with blood from the other side. As a result, not enough oxygen and nutrients reach the body's cells, resulting in shortness of breath, tiredness, heart failure, and even a stroke. Sometimes, these holes close naturally, but an operation may be needed.

Blood flow

The blood circulates, or flows, around the body in a system of blood vessels called the vascular network. Arteries take blood away from the heart, veins bring it back again, and tiny vessels called capillaries connect the arteries and veins.

Two systems

Just as the heart is two pumps, the circulation has two parts. The arteries and veins that lead to and from the left side of the heart are known as the systemic circulation. The systemic arteries deliver oxygen, energy, nutrients, and other important substances to the body's billions of microscopic cells. The systemic veins then collect waste products.

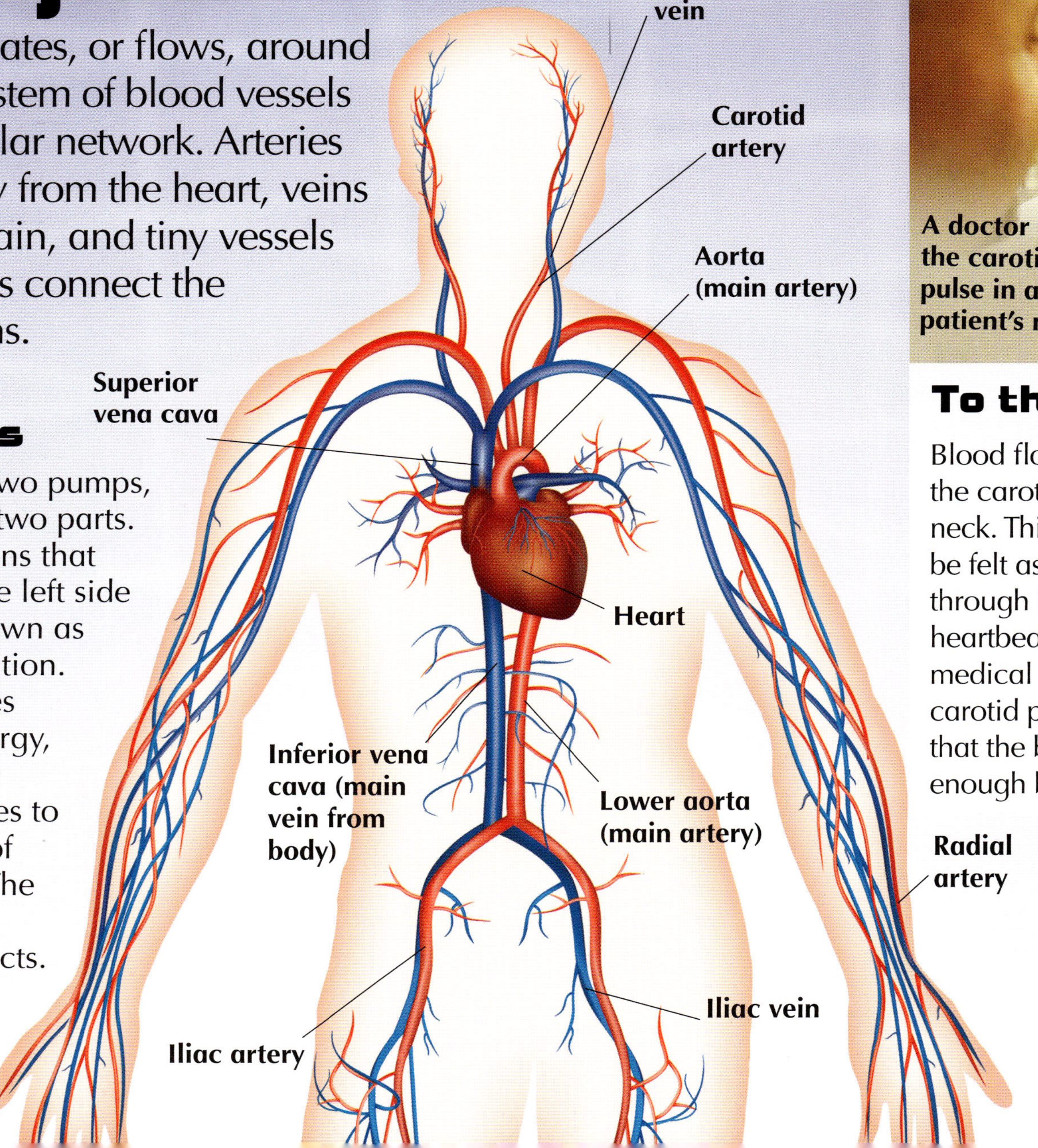

Jugular vein

Carotid artery

Aorta (main artery)

Superior vena cava

Heart

Inferior vena cava (main vein from body)

Lower aorta (main artery)

Radial artery

Iliac artery

Iliac vein

MAIN BLOOD VESSELS OF THE CIRCULATION

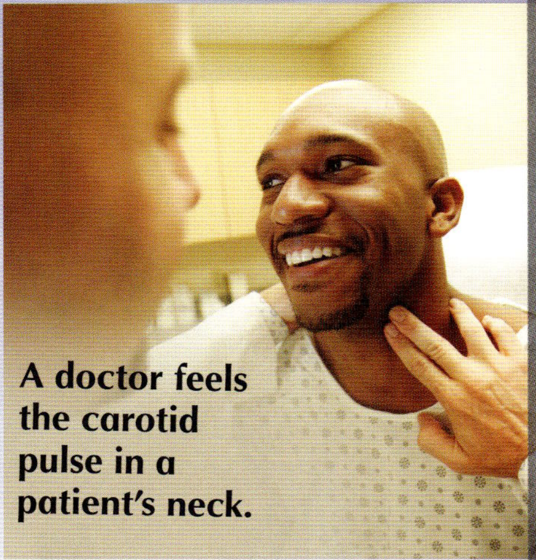

A doctor feels the carotid pulse in a patient's neck.

To the brain

Blood flows to the brain up the carotid artery in the neck. This artery's pulse can be felt as blood surges through it with each heartbeat. In an emergency, medical staff check the carotid pulse to make sure that the brain is receiving enough blood.

After exercise, we have to stop to allow our bodies to recover.

Exhausted

During exercise, the muscles need more oxygen and energy, so the heart beats faster to supply more blood. After exercising for a while, the circulation cannot keep up. We have to slow down and breathe faster and deeper to take in more oxygen, which allows the circulation to settle down again.

Lungs and oxygen

The second set of arteries and veins takes blood from the right side of the heart to the lungs for more oxygen. This system is called the pulmonary circulation. As the blood leaves the heart, it is low in oxygen and dark reddish-blue. In the lungs, the blood absorbs oxygen, turns bright red, and flows back to the left side of the heart.

DiscoveryFact™

If all your blood vessels could be taken out of your body and laid end to end, they would stretch 62,000 miles. This is the same distance as two-and-a-half times around the earth!

Did you know?

- **It takes a drop of blood one minute to travel around the entire systemic circulation.**
- **The time taken for one drop to pass through the pulmonary circulation is less than ten seconds.**
- **In the systemic circulation, arteries carry bright red, oxygen-rich blood.**
- **In the pulmonary circulation, the arteries carry dark reddish-blue blood that is low in oxygen.**

Blood cells

An adult has about 5 quarts of blood in his or her body. This thick, red, sticky fluid is essential to life—without it we would die. It does many vital jobs, including carrying oxygen around the body, removing waste, and fighting disease.

A magnified image of red blood cells

Red blood cells

Blood consists of billions of microscopic cells floating in a liquid called plasma. There are three main kinds of cells: the most numerous are red blood cells, also known as erythrocytes. They are shaped like doughnuts without the holes, and their main task is to take in oxygen from the lungs and release it to the organs and tissues.

DiscoveryFact™

A tiny drop of blood as small as a pinhead contains approximately 5 million red blood cells, 10,000 white blood cells, and 300,000 platelets.

Plasma: 55%

White blood cells and platelets: 4%

Red blood cells: 41%

What's in blood?

More than half of blood is liquid plasma, which is mostly water. Plasma also contains nutrients, glucose, hormones, and hundreds of other substances. The red and white cells and the platelets move around in the liquid plasma.

Other blood cells

The second kind of blood cells are white blood cells, known as leukocytes. These cells fight germs and disease and remove waste from the blood and body. The third kind of cells are platelets, also called thrombocytes. These are more like cell fragments, and their major task is to help blood clot in cuts and wounds to form a scab.

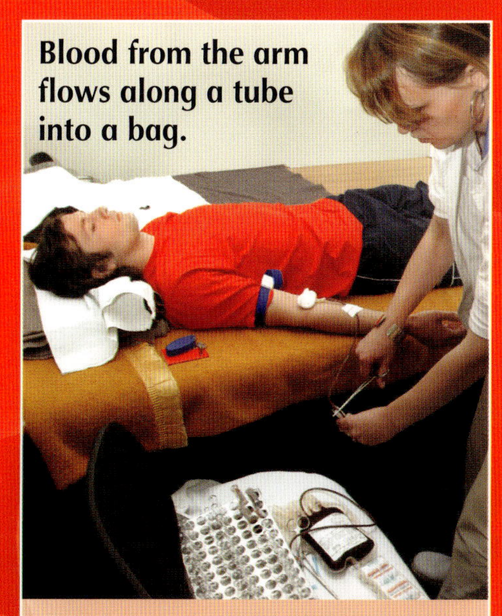

Blood from the arm flows along a tube into a bag.

Giving blood

Many people donate, or give, blood. The body makes up the lost blood in a few days. Giving blood saves millions of lives around the world every year.

Blood groups

In 1901, Austrian doctor Karl Landsteiner realized that not all blood is the same. Different people have blood from different groups. These groups are labeled A, B, AB, and O. If blood of the wrong group is given to a person, it can kill them.

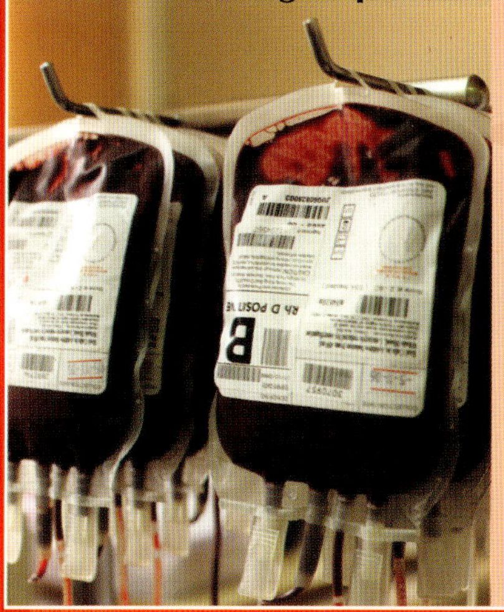

Bags of donated blood are labeled according to their blood group.

Storing blood

Donated blood is tested for infections and to find out its blood group. It is then stored in a blood bank, ready to be used if someone needs it during an operation or because of an accident. The blood is transfused, or passed, into the patient through a tube connected to a vein.

Blood vessels

When blood leaves the heart, it passes through strong, thick-walled arteries. These split and branch many times to form tiny capillaries, which then join to the veins that carry the blood back to the heart.

To the heart

The blood flowing through the veins is under low pressure. As veins approach the heart, they get wider and wider until they pour into two very large veins. These are the superior vena cava, which brings blood from the head and arms, and the inferior vena cava, which brings blood from the legs and trunk (see pages 50–51).

Varicose veins

Varicose veins are veins that look like twisted lumps under the skin. They are caused by the vein walls becoming weak and the veins widening. This means that the valves cannot work properly and they allow blood to flow the wrong way. Compare this with the diagram of a properly working vein on page 47. As the blood flows the wrong way, it makes the veins bulge and forms bumps on the skin.

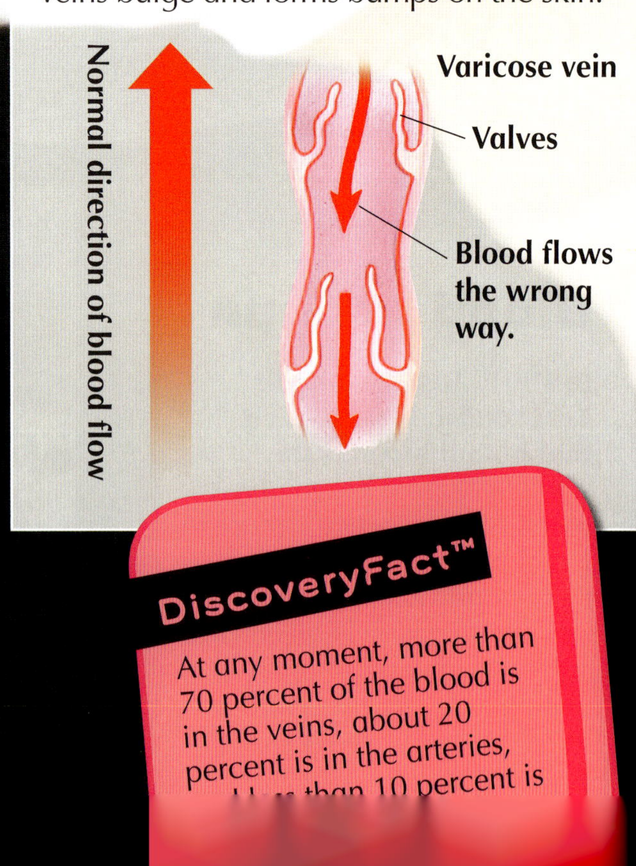

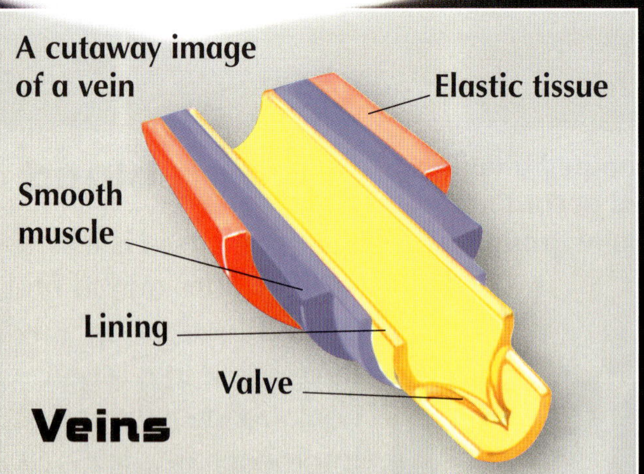

Veins

The wall of a vein has thin layers of smooth muscle. These muscles contract to keep the blood moving toward the heart. In many of the larger veins, the inner lining has flaps that act as valves, which stop the blood from going the wrong way.

DiscoveryFact™

At any moment, more than 70 percent of the blood is in the veins, about 20 percent is in the arteries,

Looking at blood vessels

- Have a look at the inside of your wrist. You can probably see blue lines under the skin.
- These are veins carrying blood from your hands. You can't usually see the arteries in the wrist because they are deeper under the skin and have thicker walls that hide the blood.

A nurse takes blood from a vein in the arm using a hollow needle.

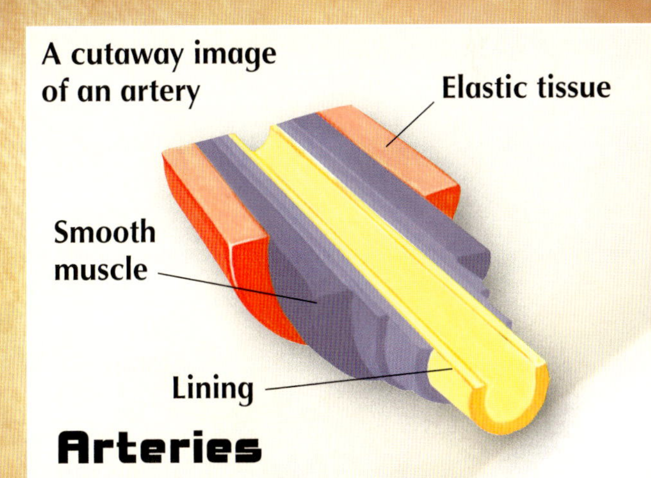

Arteries

An artery's wall has several layers: the inner layer is a smooth lining along which blood flows, the middle layer is muscle, and the outer layer is elastic tissue. The muscles contract to squeeze the artery, pushing the blood along.

From the heart

Blood is pumped from the heart under great pressure. Arteries have thicker walls than veins to withstand this high blood pressure without bursting. They also have layers of muscles in their walls that can tighten to make the artery narrower. The brain controls the width of the arteries, allowing it to alter the amount of blood that flows to each body part.

Quick Quiz

Are these sentences TRUE or FALSE?
Place the correct sticker in the box.

1. The heart pumps about 5 quarts of blood each minute.
2. The heart has three inner chambers.
3. It takes a drop of blood 30 minutes to travel around the entire systematic circulation.
4. More than half of blood is liquid plasma.
5. Varicose veins are veins that appear as twisted lumps under the skin.

Find the stickers to finish the diagrams.

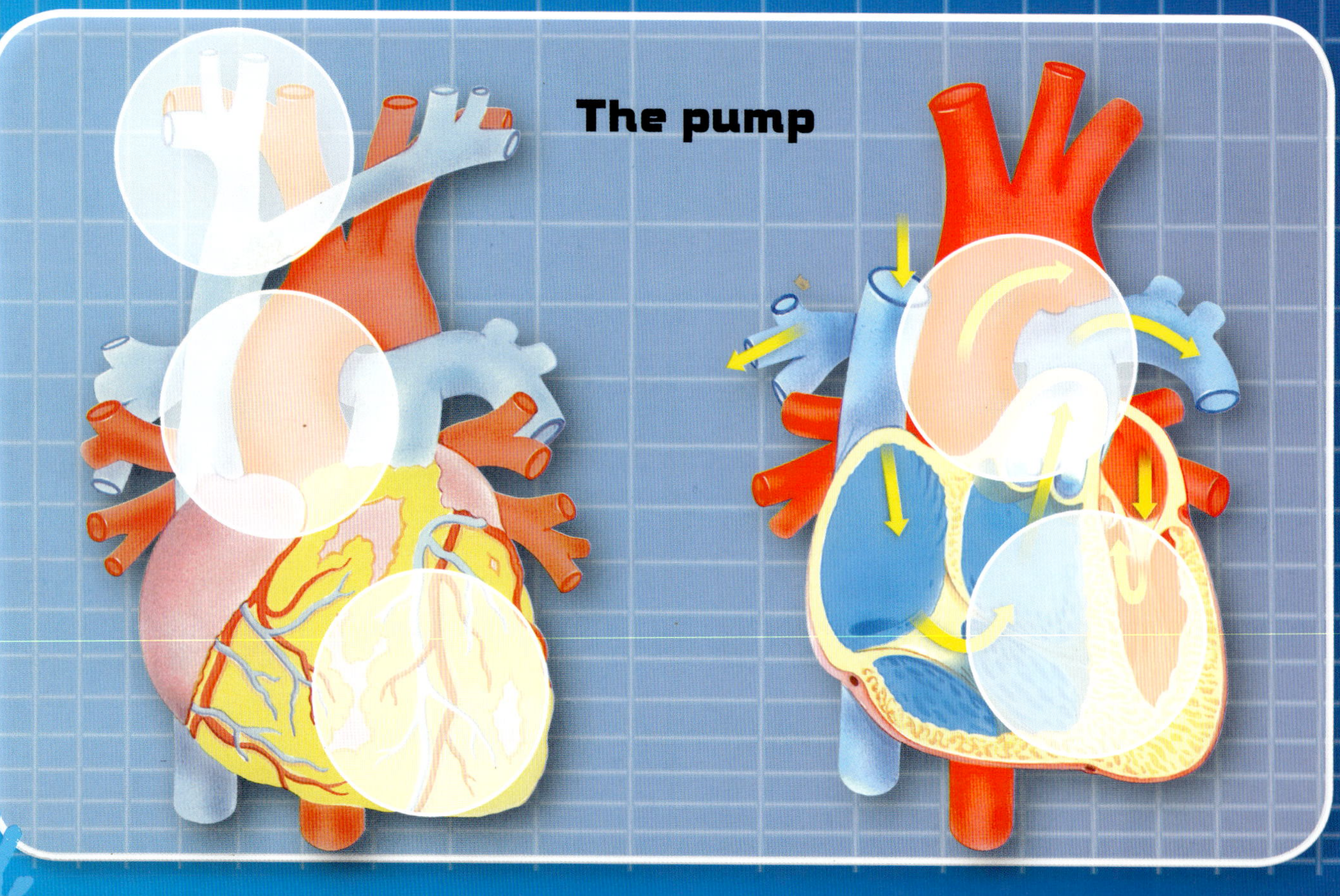

ANSWERS: 1 – T, 2 – F, 3 – F, 4 – T, 5 –T

Food and digestion

Why do we need food? It gives us energy for our muscles as we move around, and it also provides energy for all the processes that happen inside our bodies. Food supplies the raw materials needed for growth in babies and children and to repair everyday wear and tear. Food is also tasty and a pleasure to eat. The parts of the body that deal with food—from the first bite to getting rid of the waste—are known as the digestive system.

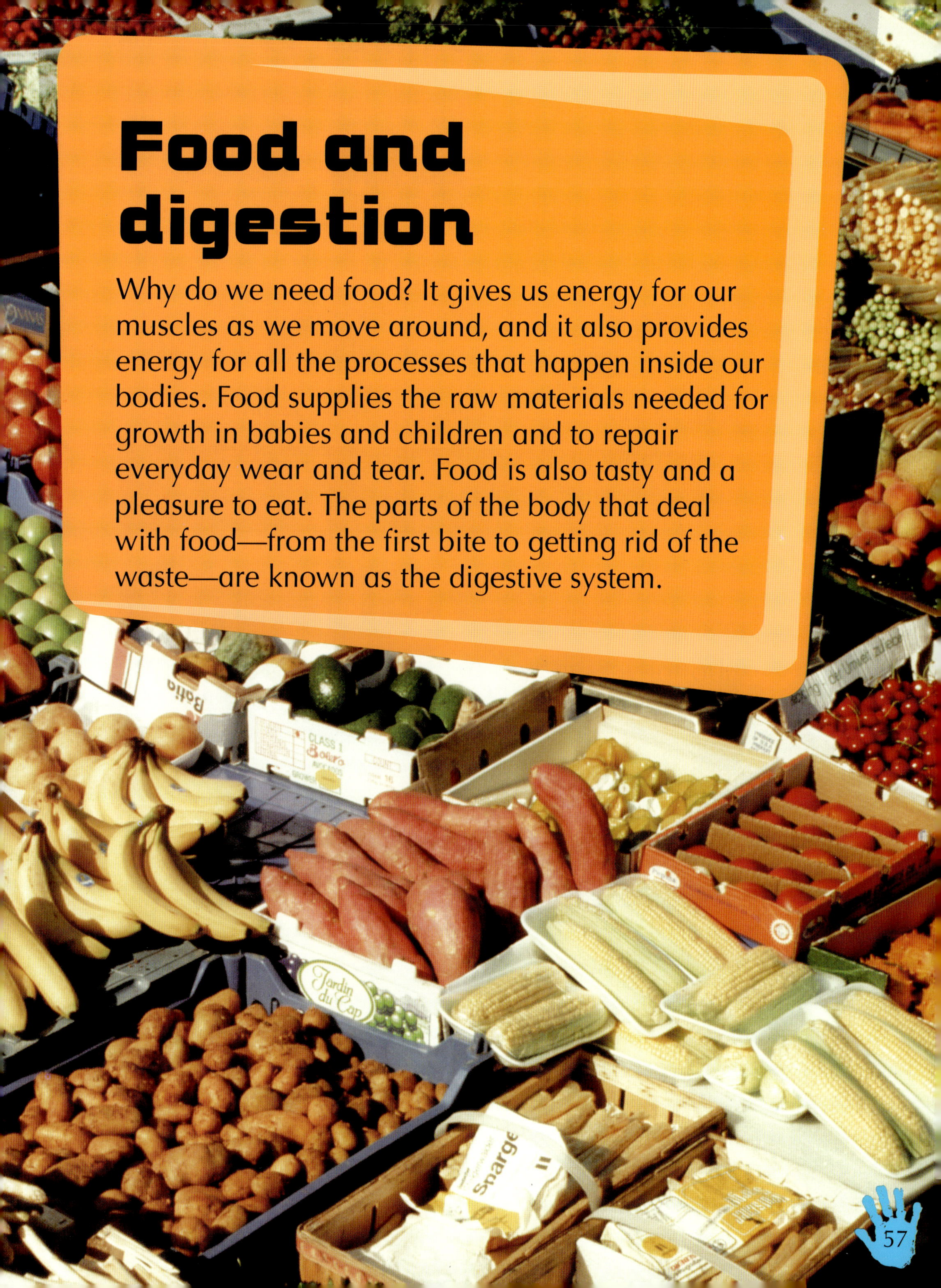

Food's journey

Swallowing is the start of a long journey for your food that takes 24 hours or more and involves traveling up to 30 feet through a dark tube full of powerful chemicals.

Digestive tract

The digestive tract is a long tube that starts at the mouth and ends at the anus. Food is chewed in the mouth, swallowed down the throat, and pushed through the esophagus, or gullet, into the stomach. It then travels through the small and large intestines to the anus, where waste is passed out.

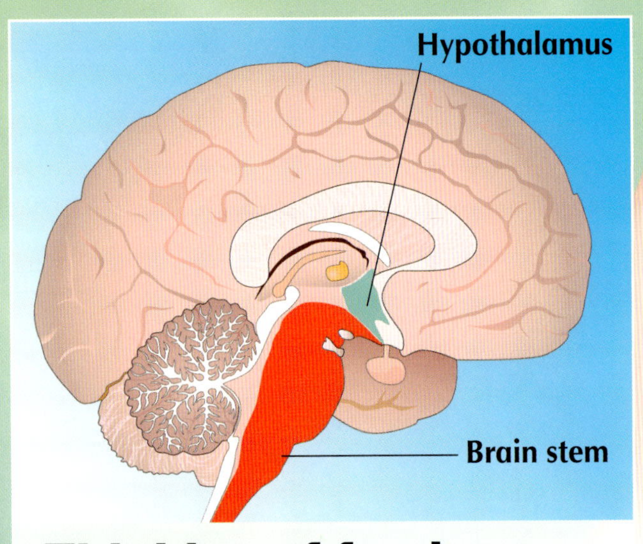

Thinking of food

The brain plays a vital role in digestion. A part called the hypothalamus makes us feel hungry and thirsty. The brain stem lies between the spinal cord and the upper brain. It controls the automatic movements of the gut and the removal of food waste.

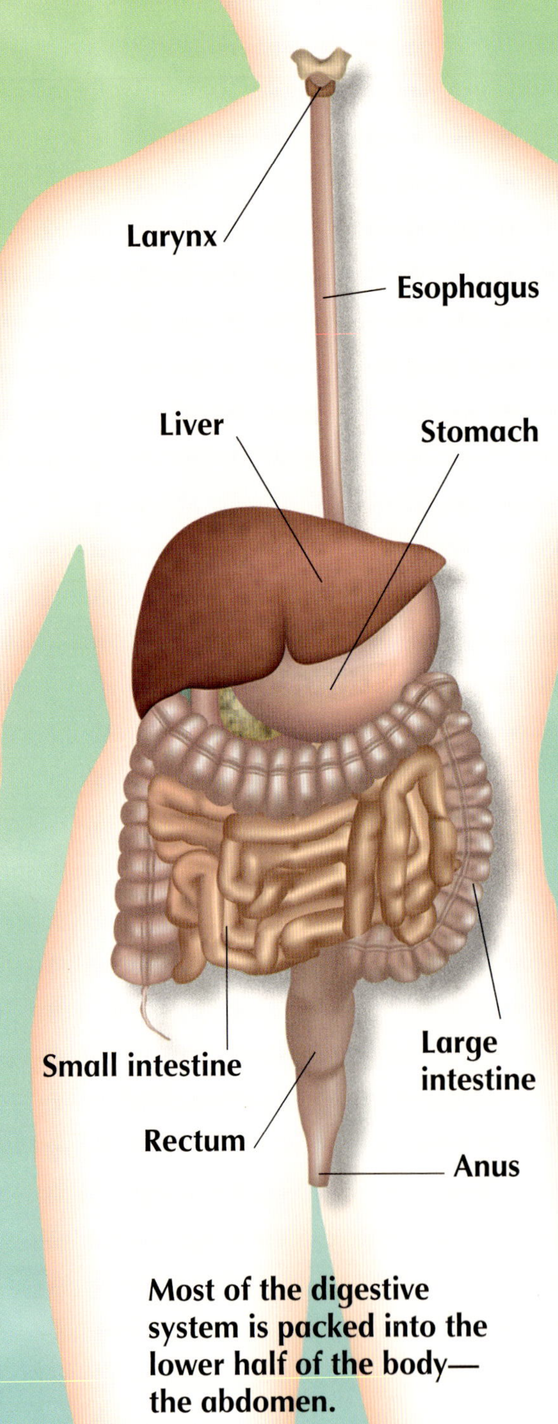

Most of the digestive system is packed into the lower half of the body—the abdomen.

Food study

In 1822, American doctor William Beaumont attended a patient who had been shot in the stomach. The small bullet hole was kept open and provided a "window" for studying what happened in the stomach. Beaumont poked into the hole and took samples of the chemicals that the stomach made after the patient ate.

Breaking down food

In the digestive tract, the food is digested, or broken down, and absorbed into the body. Anything that isn't absorbed or used by the body is expelled as waste. Several other body parts help with the digestion of food, including the liver and pancreas. They create some of the chemicals needed to break down and absorb food.

Water

As well as food, the body also needs water. Water is essential for almost every process in the body—from digestion to sweating. Some water is contained in food, but everyone should also drink plenty of water.

The body needs water to survive.

Big eater

Elephants have huge bodies, which need a lot of energy. They eat mainly grass, leaves, and other plant foods that are low in nourishment. So to get enough energy from its diet, an adult elephant must eat for about 18 to 20 hours every day. An elephant can eat more than 440 pounds of plant food daily, which is about the weight of three adult humans.

An elephant grasps food with its trunk and chews with its huge teeth.

DiscoveryFact™

In a year, an adult human needs to eat more than half a ton of food. That's half the weight of a small car. An adult also needs to drink about 185 gallons of water—enough to fill 50 bathtubs.

What's in food?

Food is not just needed to fill us up and ward off hunger. It contains hundreds of substances that your body must have to stay fit and healthy and to work well.

The right balance

The body needs the right balance of different types of food. Too much of any single food item can cause harm. A healthy balance contains plenty of fruit and vegetables, grains such as bread, pasta, and rice, some fish and dairy products, and not too much meat—especially red meat. Foods that are high in sugar and fats should be eaten only in small quantities.

This food pyramid shows the proportions of each type of food you should eat in a healthy diet.

Fats

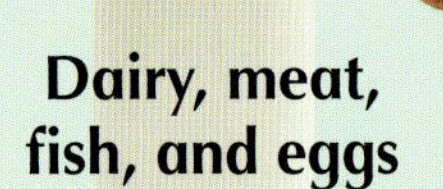

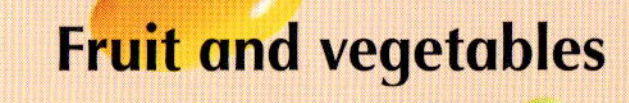

Grains: bread, pasta, rice, and cereal

DiscoveryFact™

Every few weeks, a new fad diet comes and goes. But the basics of healthy eating have been the same since people lived in caves!

Food for energy

Different foods contain a variety of substances, and they all perform different roles once they have been absorbed by the body. For example, vitamins and minerals help to keep the body working well. Proteins are important for building new cells and tissue, as well as repairing damaged ones. Carbohydrates are used to supply the energy we need to live.

Fresh fruit contains a lot of vitamins and minerals.

Vitamins and minerals

There are many vitamins and minerals that are important to your body. For example, vitamin C helps to keep your gums healthy, while vitamin D helps to keep your bones strong. The mineral iron is important for healthy blood.

Protein

Meat, fish, eggs, nuts, legumes, and cheese contain a lot of protein. Your body breaks down the protein you eat into simpler chemicals called amino acids. It can then use these amino acids to build new proteins to make and repair body cells.

Meat and fish contain a lot of protein.

Did you know?

- **An important part of food, which the body does not digest, is fiber. Fiber helps the intestines to stay healthy. Fruit and vegetables and whole foods—in which every part of the grain is used—contain a lot of fiber.**
- **Processed foods have been changed so much that they lose some of their natural goodness. White bread, for example, has very little fiber left.**

Bread contains a lot of carbohydrates.

Carbohydrates

Sugar and starch are foods that contain a lot of carbohydrates. While your body needs these substances to make energy, if you eat too many carbohydrates, your body turns them into fat. It then stores this fat in a layer just under the skin called the adipose tissue.

Teeth and biting

Teeth bite, grind, and chew food to make it easier to swallow and digest. They are coated with enamel—the hardest material in the body—so that they last a long time. In fact, you will only have two sets of teeth throughout your entire lifetime!

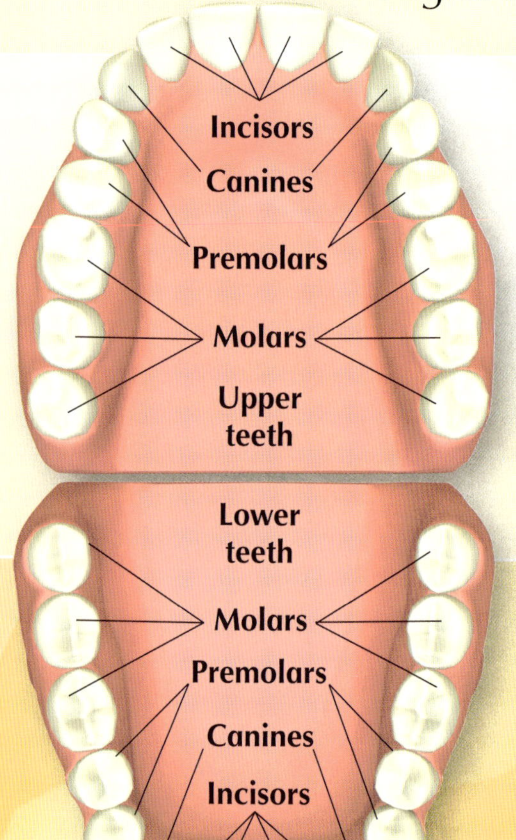

The full set

An adult has 32 teeth. There are four different types of teeth: 8 incisors at the front, 4 canines next to them, 8 premolars, and 12 molars at the rear of the mouth.

Eating an apple would be difficult without teeth.

Baby teeth

How many teeth you have depends partly on your age. Babies have none or very few teeth. Then, small "baby," or milk, teeth appear, with most children having a full set of 20 baby teeth by about the age of three or four. From around six or seven years old, these teeth start to fall out and are replaced by adult ones.

Look at your tooth prints

- Choose a crunchy fruit, such as an apple, and bite into it with your front teeth to take out a lump.
- Look at the tooth prints in the area you have bitten. Can you see the separate tooth marks and the curve of the teeth in your jaws?
- Ask some friends to do the same and compare your tooth prints.

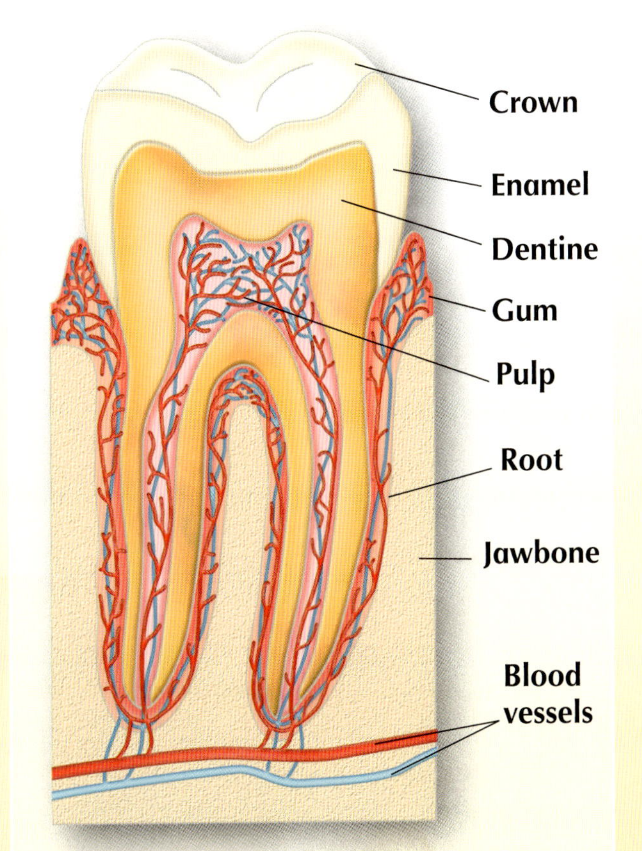

Uses for teeth

Teeth are like tools and have different shapes for different tasks. The chisel-like incisors at the front have straight, narrow edges for biting and slicing food. The canines, or eyeteeth, next to the incisors are tall and pointed to tear and rip. The premolars and molars, or cheek teeth, are broad and flat with rounded humps for crushing and chewing.

Inside a tooth

A tooth has two parts: the crown above the gum and the roots below. The top layer of the crown is made of enamel. Beneath this is dentine, which is also a very tough material, and in the middle is the soft pulp. Blood vessels supply the tooth with nutrients.

DiscoveryFact™

The four molars at the back of the mouth are the last teeth to appear, at about 17 to 20 years of age. Because they grow in adulthood, they are known as "wisdom teeth." In some people, they never appear—perhaps because there is not enough room.

Hunter's teeth

Lions and other hunting animals have very large, pointed canine teeth for stabbing into prey and ripping flesh. Lions also have sharp-edged molar teeth called carnassials for cutting into tough meat.

In the stomach

Swallowed food takes a few seconds to travel down the esophagus. It is pushed into the baglike stomach, which attacks the food with powerful acids, enzymes, and other chemicals.

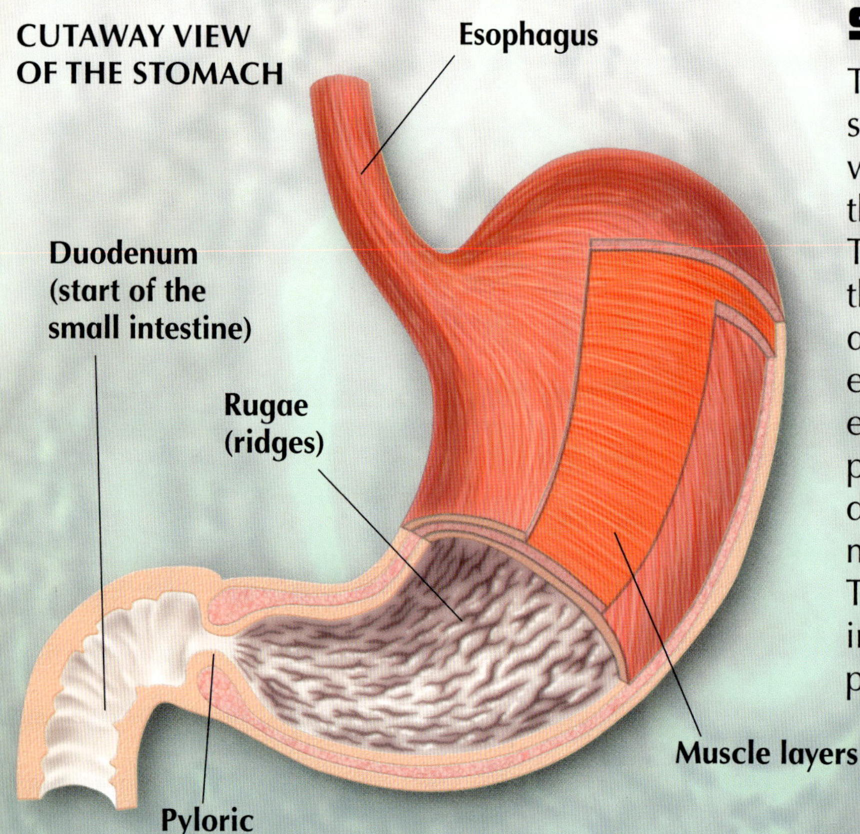

Stomach wall

The stomach is a large bag that sits just below the left lung. Its walls have several layers—three of these are made of muscle fibers. The muscles tighten and contract the stomach to squash, mix, and mash the food inside. The entrance to the stomach from the esophagus and the exit into the part of the intestine called the duodenum both have rings of muscle fibers known as sphincters. These stay closed to keep the food in the stomach until it is ready to pass into the intestines.

Stomach wall

The inside of the stomach wall is folded into ridges called rugae, which allow the stomach to stretch. The innermost layer of the stomach wall is the mucosa. The next layer is the tough and stretchy submucosa. The three muscle layers are next, forming the outside of the stomach.

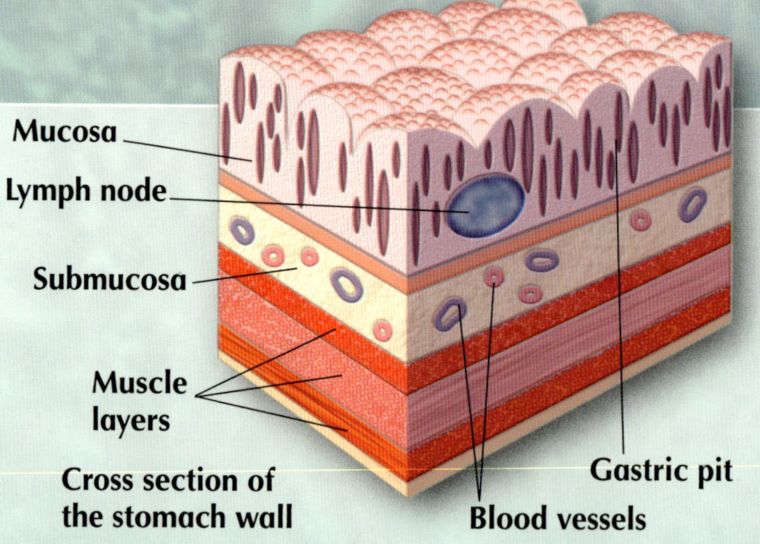

Cross section of the stomach wall

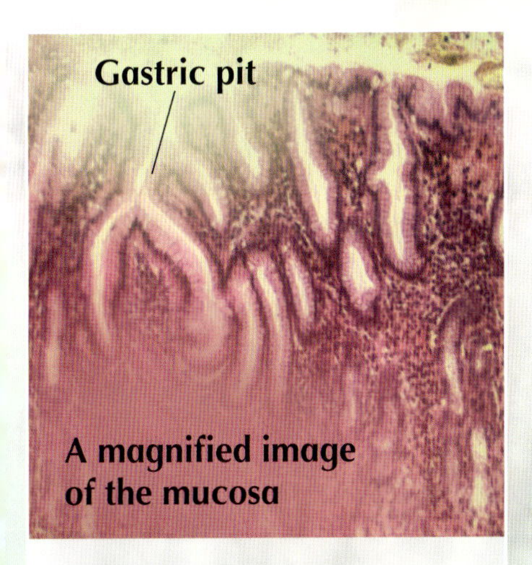

A magnified image of the mucosa

Warning! Acid!

Hydrochloric acid is an extremely strong chemical. It is over ten times more powerful than the acidic juices found in vinegar and lemon.

Gastric pits

The mucosa has thousands of gastric pits. These are lined with cells that make a wide range of chemicals, including slimy mucus, hydrochloric acid, and the enzyme pepsin.

Stomach juices

Apart from mashing the food physically, the stomach also attacks the food with powerful chemicals. Its lining produces a strong acid called hydrochloric acid. The lining also makes more of the chemicals called enzymes. These get to work breaking down different parts of the meal. For example, lipase attacks fatty foods and pepsin breaks down proteins.

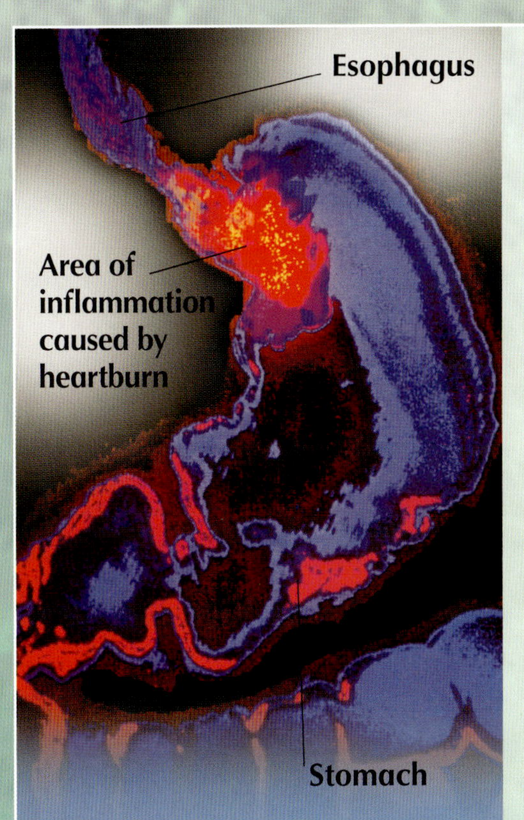

Heartburn

In some people, the contents of the stomach seep back up into the esophagus, or lower gullet. This causes inflammation and pain in the chest, where the acid attacks the gullet lining. The pain is known as heartburn, although it has nothing to do with the heart.

An image showing inflammation caused by stomach contents entering the esophagus.

Did you know?

- **Your stomach begins to contract and produce juices as soon as you see or smell food.**
- **An adult stomach can hold up to 4 pints of food and beverages.**
- **Most food stays in the stomach for one to four hours.**
- **Fatty foods stay in the stomach for longer.**

Guts galore

After a few hours in the stomach, even the most beautiful-looking meal has become a thick, dark, mushy "soup." However, there is more digestion to come in the next part of the digestive tract—the small intestine.

Gut pioneer

In 1780, Italian scientist Lazzaro Spallanzani wrote a book about digestion. He did many experiments on his own digestive system, such as swallowing food in net bags on long pieces of string and pulling them back up to see what had happened. *Don't try this at home!*

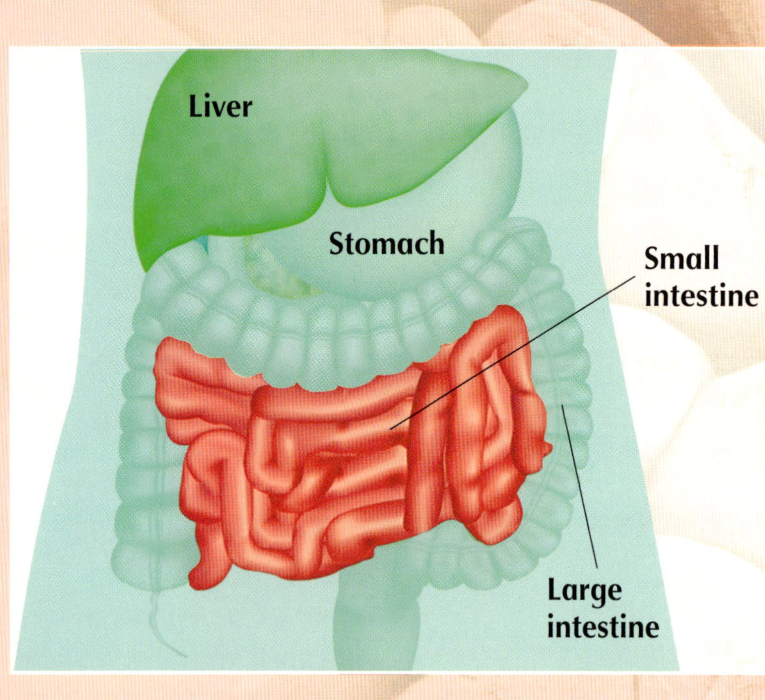

Small intestine

The small intestine, or small bowel, is a narrow but very long tube. It has three parts: first, the duodenum, which is the shortest section; then the middle section, the jejunum; and finally the longest section, the ileum, which connects to the large intestine. The small intestine is coiled, looped, and folded into the middle of the lower body and is almost surrounded by the next part of the digestive tract, the large intestine.

More digestion

The small intestine contains many more enzymes that attack food and continue breaking it into smaller pieces. Most of these enzymes are not made in the small intestine but come from another digestive organ called the pancreas, which is found in the left side of the body under the stomach.

A microscopic image of the villi in the lining of the small intestine.

Intestine lining

The small intestine has many folds in its lining. The folds are made of millions of tiny fingerlike parts called villi. Each single villus has a system of tiny vessels inside—some are for blood, but a larger one, the lacteal, is for the fluid known as lymph. Nutrients pass into the blood and the lymph. The folds and villi give a huge surface area for absorbing nutrients.

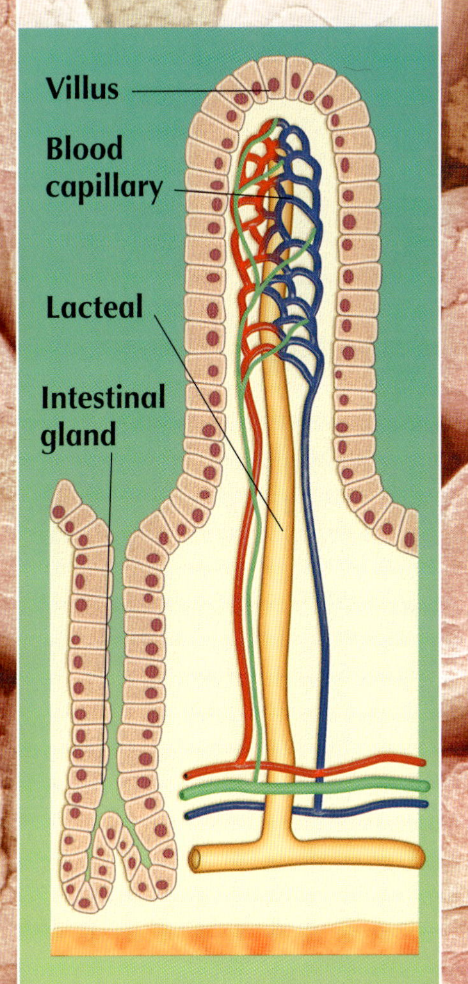

Soaking up nutrients

As food reaches its last stages of digestion, the small intestine has another job—it soaks up, or absorbs, the resulting nutrients. These nutrients are small enough to seep through the lining of the small intestine into the blood, which carries them away to the liver.

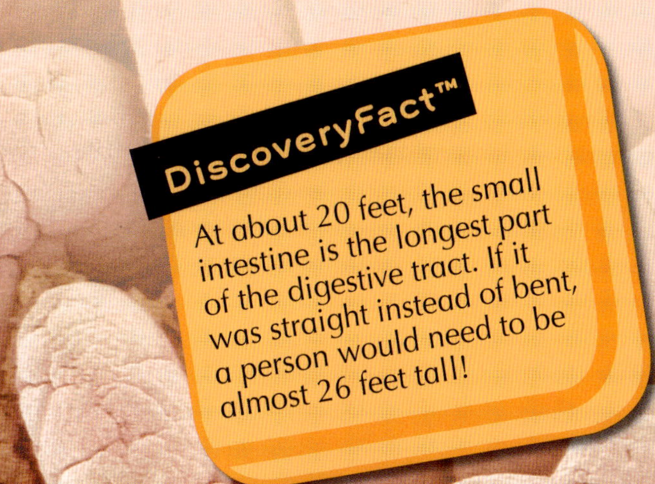

Digestion

The diagram on the right shows approximately how long food spends in each part of the intestine. During the food's travels through the guts, different enzymes break down different types of food. For example, only carbohydrates are broken down in the mouth. Carbohydrates and proteins are broken down in the stomach, while fats are mainly broken down in the small intestine.

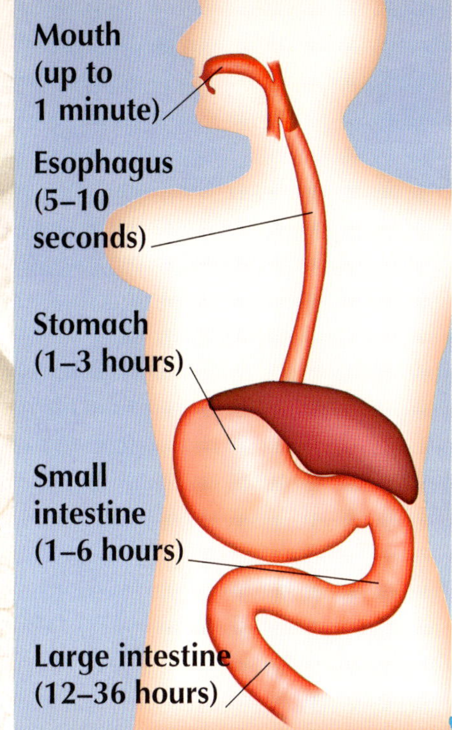

On the way out

After digestion and absorption in the small intestine, the next part of the digestive tract is the large intestine. Its main tasks are to take a few more nutrients from the remaining digested food and to remove as much water as the body needs. The waste matter is then ready for removal.

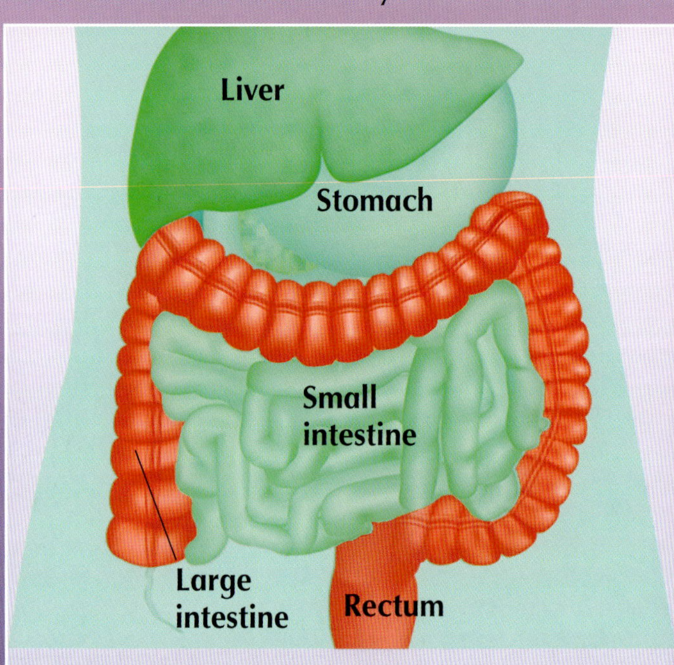

Large intestine

At about 5 feet long, the large intestine is much shorter than the small intestine, but it is wider—2 to 2½ inches wide. It forms a type of frame around the abdomen with the small intestine inside it. The large intestine is sometimes called the colon. Its strong muscles push the partly digested food along by contracting and relaxing, creating pulses of movement. The large intestine lining is coated in mucus that lubricates the inside and helps the food move smoothly.

Tiny helpers

The large intestine contains millions of tiny helpers—minute living things of various kinds, mainly bacteria. These microbes are "friendly" and work with the body. They can digest some things that the body cannot, such as certain plant foods. The microbes use some of these digested products, while the body absorbs the rest. The gut provides the microbes with a safe, warm, moist, food-filled place to live.

Did you know?

- **In an average person, more than a half of the feces, or solid waste, is water. Much of the rest is undigested food material, such as fiber.**
- **The brown color of feces is due to a substance called bilirubin that comes from the breakdown of old red blood cells in the liver.**

Inside the large intestine

This X-ray picture was taken after a substance called barium was put into the gut. The barium shows up white on X-rays and makes the colon easier to see.

The final stage

The last part of the large intestine is a short, wide tube called the rectum. Feces collect there before they are finally squeezed out through the anus. This double-ring of muscles loosens to allow the feces to leave during emptying of the bowels, known as defecation.

Treating waste

From the bathroom, bodily waste goes through the sewage system to a waste treatment plant. The waste is smelly and can cause disease, so it is treated at the plant to make it harmless.

Tanks of waste at a waste treatment plant

Young children have no control over going to the bathroom, but it is something they learn as they grow up.

Quick Quiz

Are these sentences TRUE or FALSE? Place the correct sticker in the box.

1. ☐ In a year, an adult human needs to eat more than half a ton of food.
2. ☐ The body does not digest fiber.
3. ☐ Candies, cakes and chips are all good sources of iron.
4. ☐ An adult stomach can hold up to 4 pints of food and beverages.
5. ☐ It only takes two hours for food to be broken down in your system.

Find an example of each food group and place the sticker in the correct column.

Fats	Sugar	Dairy	Fruit and vegetables	Grains

ANSWERS: 1 – T, 2 – T, 3 – F, 4 – T, 5 – F

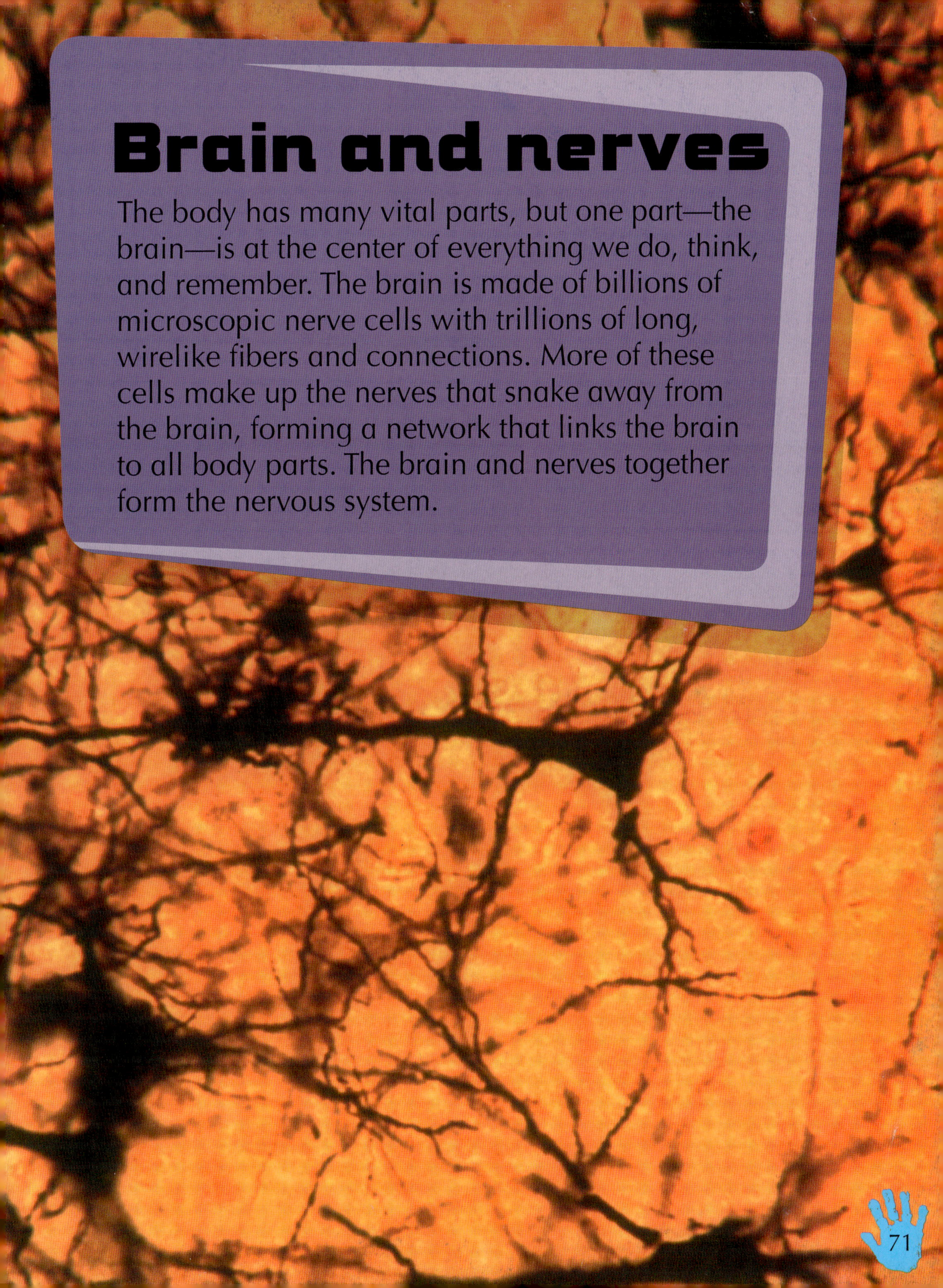

Brain and nerves

The body has many vital parts, but one part—the brain—is at the center of everything we do, think, and remember. The brain is made of billions of microscopic nerve cells with trillions of long, wirelike fibers and connections. More of these cells make up the nerves that snake away from the brain, forming a network that links the brain to all body parts. The brain and nerves together form the nervous system.

The brain

The brain, perhaps the most precious body part, is soft and slightly floppy—somewhat like a pink-gray jello. It is protected against damage by a hard skull bone and by a special cushioning fluid.

Meninges and fluid

The brain sits inside the skull and takes up the top half of the head. Inside the skull, three soft membranes called meninges wrap around the brain. Between the inner two meninges is a layer of liquid known as cerebrospinal fluid, or CSF. Together, the meninges and fluid form a soft cushion around the brain.

Did you know?

- The cushioning fluid flows around and inside the brain.
- There are four fluid-filled chambers called ventricles in the brain.
- The total amount of the cushioning fluid is about 1/2 cup.

Exterior surface of brain

Cranium (dome of skull bone)

CUTAWAY VIEW OF THE SKULL SHOWING THE BRAIN AND THE FOUR LOBES OF THE CEREBRUM (see page 74)

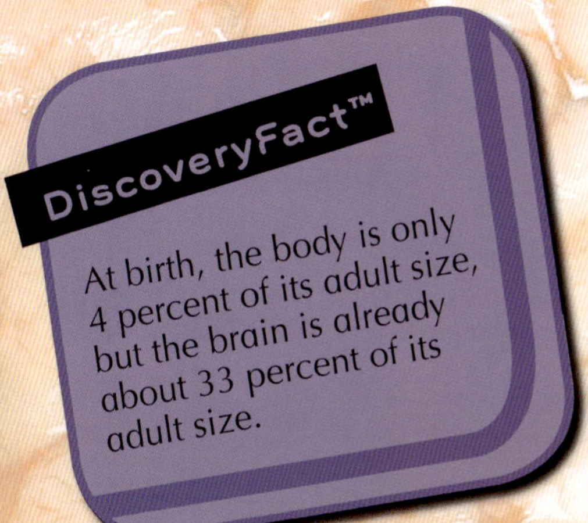

Paramedics treat a boy who has been hit on the head and is unconscious.

Knockout

Someone who has been knocked out, or made unconscious, by a blow to the head does not respond or make any movements and seems to be asleep. There may be a brain injury that will require emergency care.

Bone dome

Over and around the brain is the dome of the skull bone called the cranium. This is very strong and guards the brain against knocks and blows. The skin and hair on the head add to this protection and stop the head and brain from getting too hot or cold.

A nurse helps this stroke patient to walk again.

Slow recovery

During a stroke, a lack of blood to the brain—perhaps caused by a blocked artery—results in brain cells dying. It may take someone a long time to recover from a stroke because the undamaged parts of the brain have to learn to take over from the damaged parts.

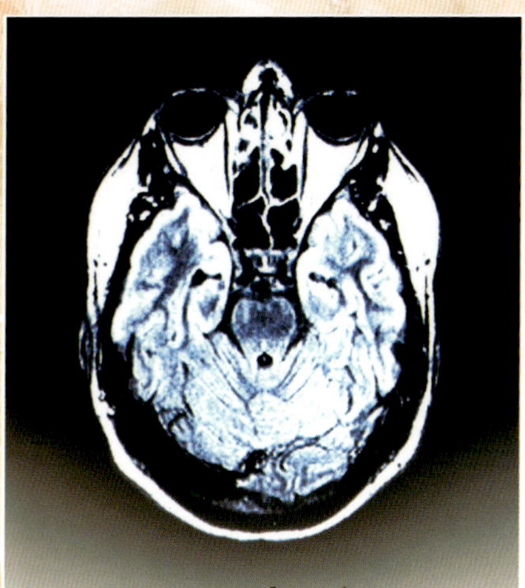
An MRI scan showing a horizontal "slice" through the middle of the brain

Seeing inside

A magnetic resonance imaging, or MRI, scanner uses magnetism and radio waves to form an image of thin layers, or slices, of the brain. The images are put together to form a picture of the whole brain to see how it works and to identify any illnesses or problems.

When studying math, the left side of the brain is very active.

Parts of the brain

The biggest part of the brain is the cerebrum—the large wrinkled dome at the top. This is where most of our thoughts, feelings, and ideas take place.

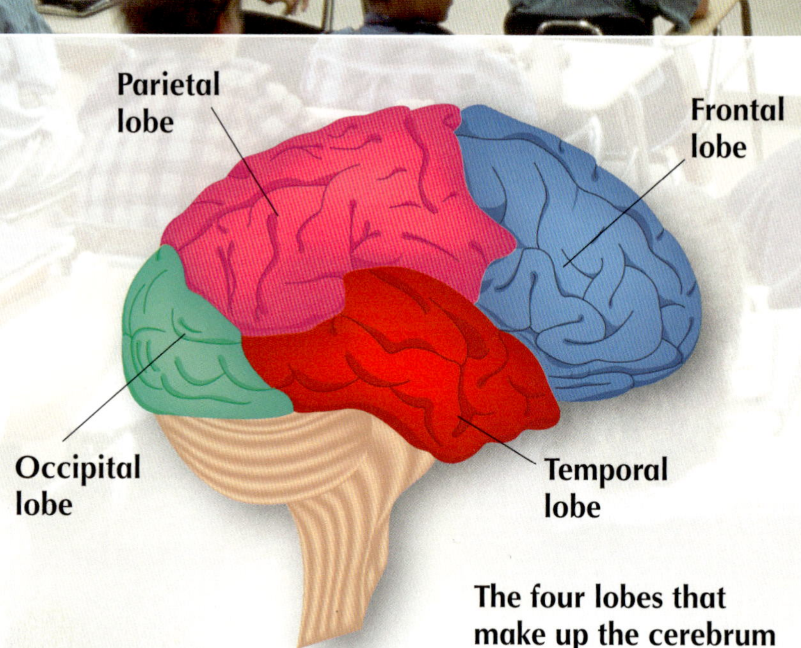

The four lobes that make up the cerebrum

On the outside

The cerebrum makes up about 90 percent of the brain. It is divided into four regions called lobes, and into left and right halves known as cerebral hemispheres. In most people, the left side of the brain is used for speaking, reading, and working out problems. The right side of the brain usually deals with more "artistic" skills, such as painting and imagination. The wrinkled surface of the cerebrum is a thin layer called the cerebral cortex.

In the middle

The center of the brain, under the cerebrum, is involved in awareness—monitoring what we see, hear, and feel. It also deals with emotions and balance and acts as a relay station. This involves passing messages between the upper and lower brain. It includes parts such as the thalamus and the hypothalamus.

The lower brain

At the lower rear of the brain is a wrinkled lump called the cerebellum. This helps to organize nerve signals going out to the muscles. It helps to make our movements smooth and skillful instead of jerky and clumsy. Like the cerebrum, the cerebellum is divided into two halves; left and right.

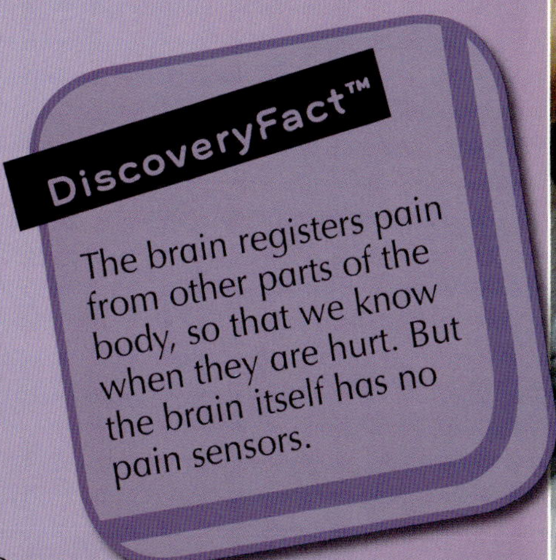

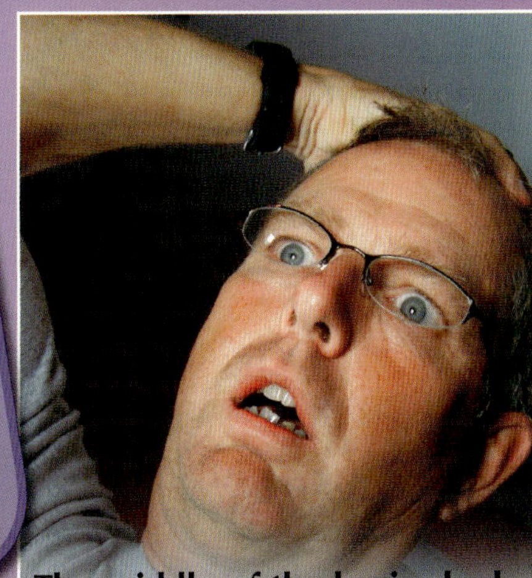

The middle of the brain deals with emotions, such as fear.

Emotions

Strong feelings, such as surprise, shock, fear, and anger, are based in the hypothalamus. This is also the area involved in powerful urges, such as thirst and hunger.

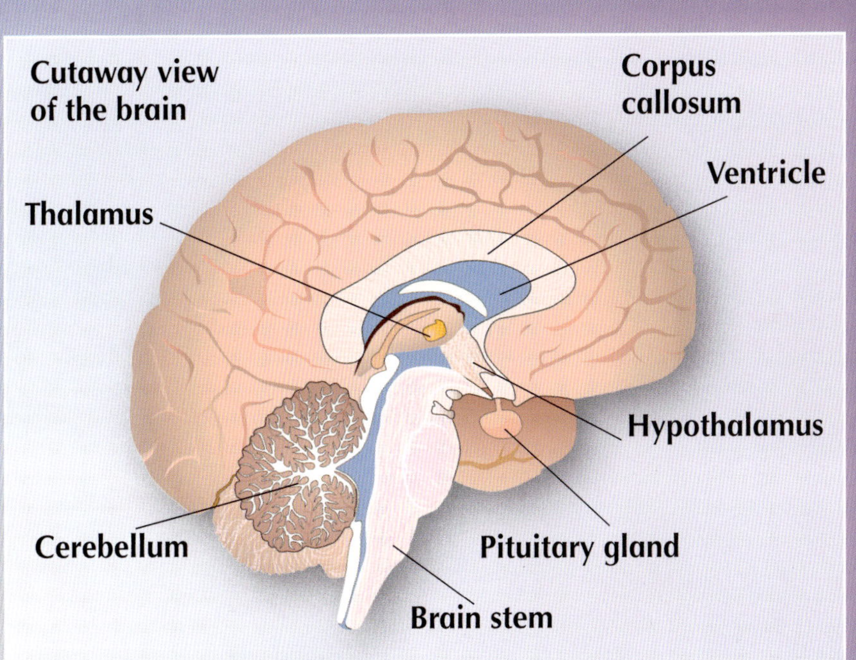

On the inside

An inside view of the brain reveals its ventricles, or fluid-filled chambers (shown above shaded in blue). Other parts include the egg-shaped thalamus and the hypothalamus, as well as the corpus callosum, which contains millions of nerve fibers that link the left and right sides of the brain. Below all of these is the brain stem, which controls many of the basic life processes, such as breathing, digestion, and blood pressure.

Did you know?

- **The average adult brain weighs 3 pounds.**
- **The largest known normal human brain weighed a whopping 6 pounds 6 ounces.**
- **Bigger brains are not necessarily smarter. There is no link between the size of a healthy brain and a person's intelligence.**

Signals

The brain and nerves contain billions of microscopic nerve cells called neurons. These cells are specialized to receive and send information as tiny pulses of electricity called nerve impulses, or nerve signals.

Nerve cells

A typical nerve cell has a wide cell body. Branching from this are many short, thin fingers called dendrites. There is usually also one longer branch called an axon, or nerve fiber. Nerve messages are picked up by the dendrites, processed and altered as they pass around the cell body, and then sent on by the axon. A motor nerve carries signals to muscles, telling them when to contract. These signals pass along the axon to the muscle fibers. Surrounding some axons is a thick, fatty protective covering called the myelin sheath.

Dendrite

Nerve cell body

Axon

Myelin sheath surrounds axon

A motor nerve cell

Muscle fibers

Electronic circuits enable computers to do millions of calculations a second.

Processing power

Nerve cells work in a similar way to the microchips in a computer. Microchips have tiny circuits inside them, along which they send electrical signals.

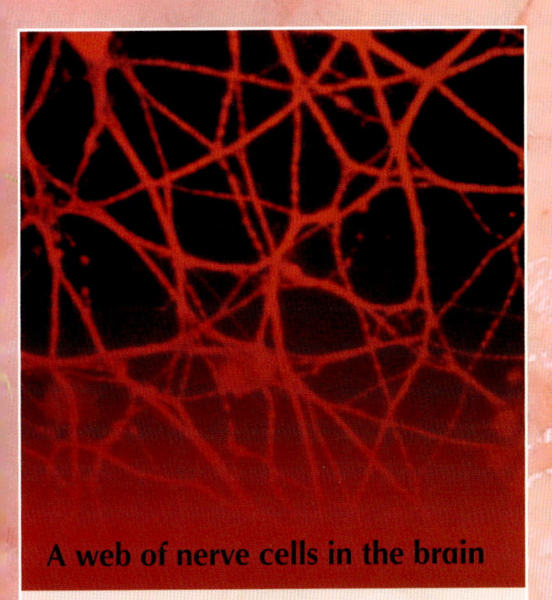
A web of nerve cells in the brain

Nerve web

The brain contains about 100 billion nerve cells. Each of these may be linked to 10,000 or more other nerve cells. The number of connections means there are trillions of pathways for signals to travel between nerve cells.

Nerve junctions

The dendrites and axons connect to the dendrites and axons of other nerve cells, but they do not actually touch each other. The junctions are separated by tiny gaps called synapses. Nerve messages "jump" across the synapse—not as electrical signals but in the form of chemicals called neurotransmitters. Each chemical "jump" takes less than a thousandth of a second.

DiscoveryFact™

Brain waves can be detected by sensors on the head, which can switch a device on or off. These sensors allow some people who are paralyzed to control devices, such as computers, just by thinking.

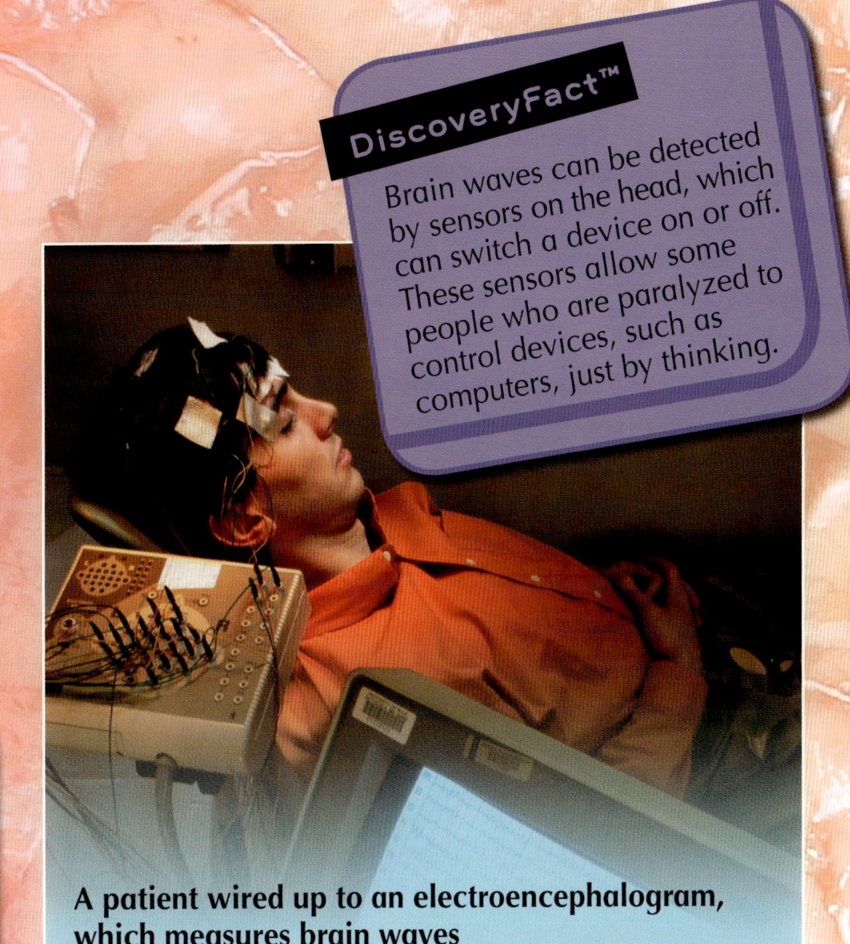
A patient wired up to an electroencephalogram, which measures brain waves

Brain waves

The brain's electrical signals can be detected by sensor pads on the head. The brain waves, or signals, can then be displayed on a screen or a paper strip as jagged wavy lines. The pattern of waves helps doctors to identify certain brain problems so that they can be treated.

Brain machine

In 1924, German physician Hans Berger invented the first machine to measure electrical signals in the human brain. In secret, he tried it out on his son Klaus, then on other people. In 1929, Berger published his first report on the brain's electrical activity.

Brain map

The outer layer of the cerebrum is called the cerebral cortex. It contains about half of the brain's nerve cells—about 50 billion—and the trillions of connections between them.

Bad accident

In 1848, American railroad worker Phineas Gage suffered a terrible injury. An iron bar passed through his frontal lobe. Before the injury, Gage was likeable but after the injury, he became difficult and short-tempered. This event started the study of how the brain is involved in personality and behavior.

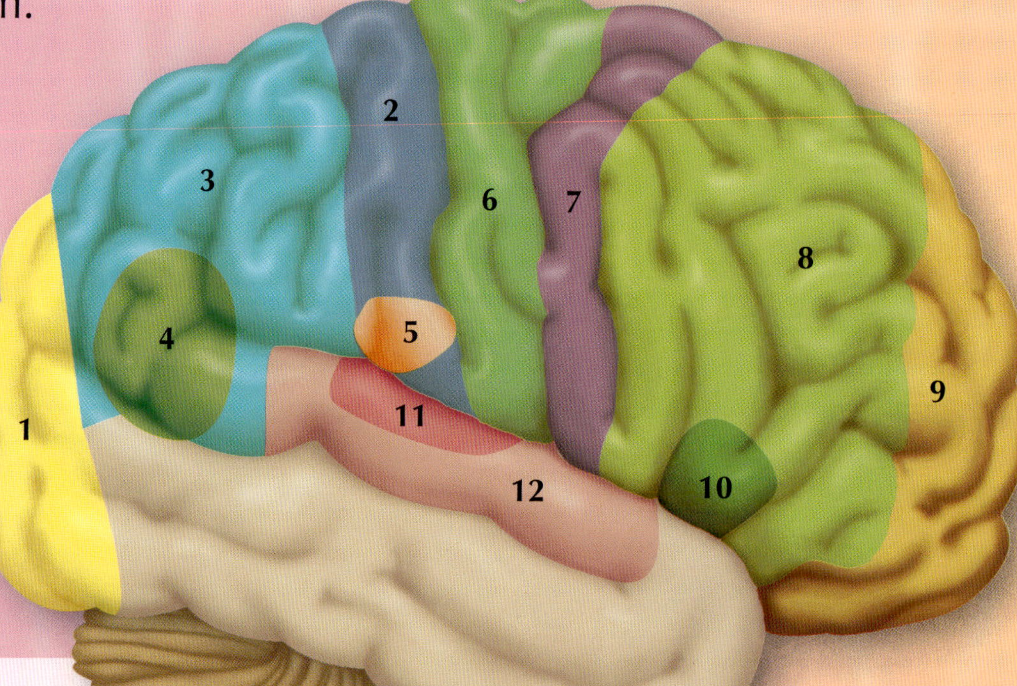

A map of the cortex

KEY TO CORTEX MAP

1. Visual area (sight)
2. Somatosensory center (touch)
3. Secondary touch area
4. Posterior (Wernicke's) speech center
5. Gustatory center (taste)
6. Motor center (organizing movements)
7. Premotor center (planning movements)
8. Frontal cortex (behavior and personality)
9. Language area (recognizing and understanding words)
10. Anterior (Broca's) speech center
11. Auditory center (hearing)
12. Vestibular center (balance)

Regions of the cortex

The cortex is the main place in the brain where we become aware of what we see, hear, smell, taste, and touch—our senses. It is also the place where we plan movements, known as motor skills, and organize them. Each of these sensory and motor processes takes place in a different area of the cortex.

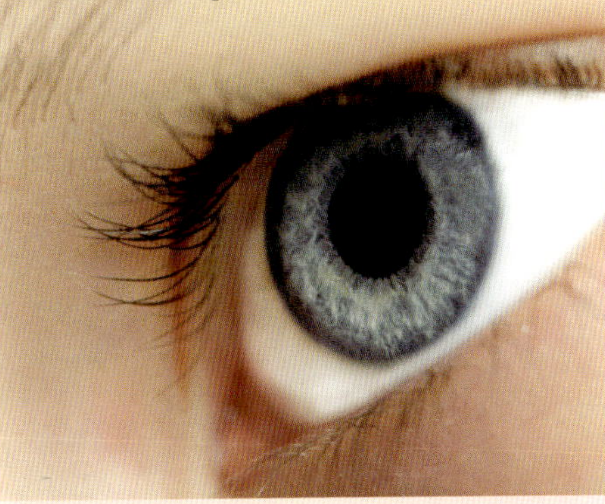

The brain interprets signals sent by the eyes and turns them into pictures.

Seeing

A person who suffers a hard blow to the lower back of the head, where the visual center is, may have sight problems and "see stars."

Hearing

Nerve signals from each ear pass along nerves to the hearing center, which is on the temporal lobe. If someone has a blow to the head in this area, they sometimes hear buzzing or scratching noises. These sounds do not come from the ear but are "made up" by the jolted brain.

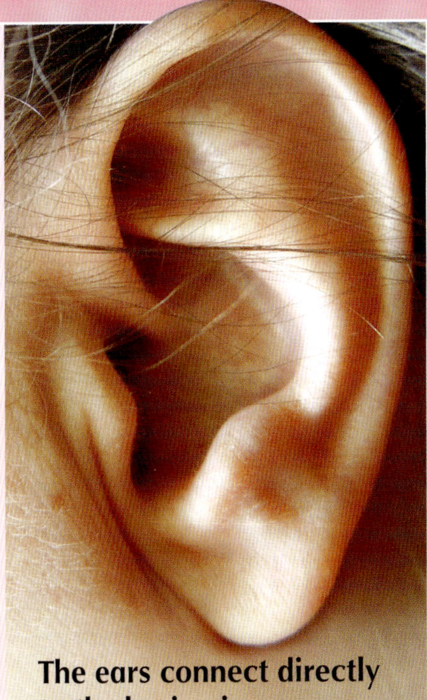

The ears connect directly to the brain via nerves.

DiscoveryFact™

If the cerebral cortex was spread out flat, it would be the size of a pillowcase and almost as thin. But its deep wrinkles allow it to fit neatly inside the head.

The mind

The cortex is the major site for thinking and for general consciousness, or awareness—what we call our "mind." The cortex is involved in learning and memory, too. It is sometimes called gray matter because all its nerve cells give it a gray color. Nerve axons from the cortex's nerve cells pass inward to the central part of the brain, where they connect to other parts, such as the thalamus and hypothalamus (see page 75).

Personality

Many parts of the brain are involved in how we behave, how we feel, and what we think. These things make us who we are—our personality. These areas include parts of the cortex, especially the frontal lobe, and the hypothalamus (see pages 74–75). The brain sends signals to your face, maybe telling it to look sad if that's how you feel.

The main nerves

Breathing is regulated by the cranial nerves. This diver is breathing underwater with the help of an oxygen tank.

The brain cannot do much by itself—it depends on nerves to link it to the rest of the body. There are 25 major nerves carrying signals between the brain, the senses, the muscles, and the glands.

Connecting nerves

The 24 cranial nerves are grouped in 12 pairs. They join the brain to various parts, mainly in the head and neck. Some carry signals to the brain and are called sensory nerves. Others carry instructions to the muscles and are called motor nerves.

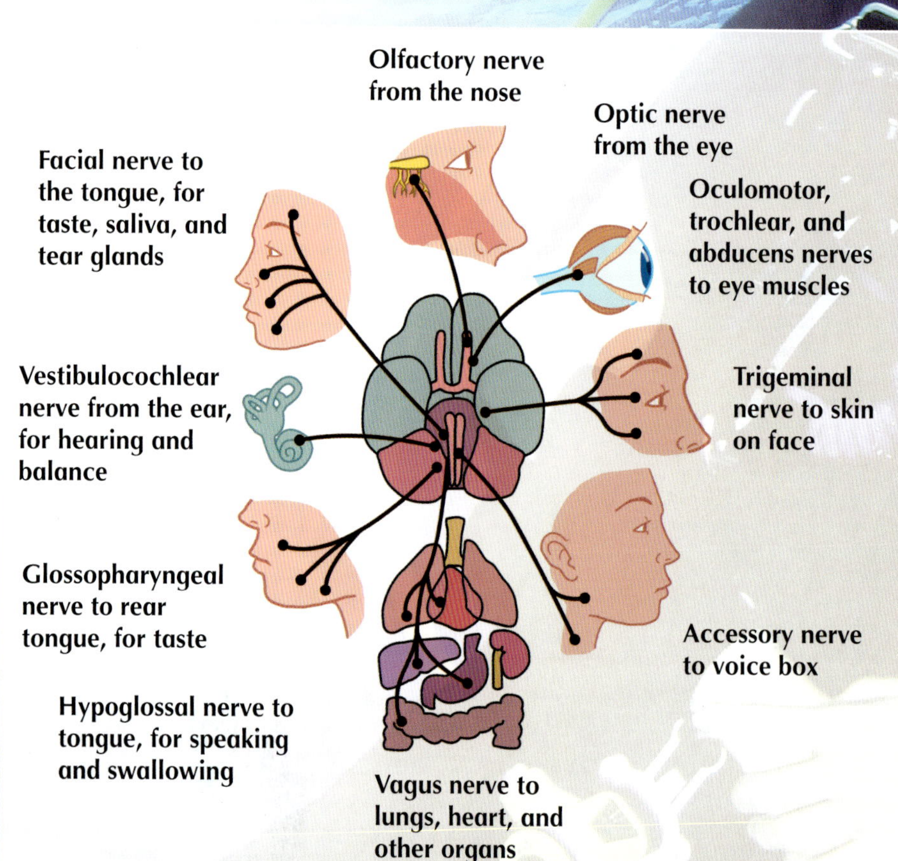

Cranial nerves

The sensory nerves bring signals to the brain from the sense organs, such as the eyes and ears. These nerves are the olfactory, the vestibulocochlear, and the optic. The motor nerves carry signals from the brain to the muscles and glands. These are the oculomotor, the trochlear, the abducens, the accessory, and the hypoglossal. Some nerves carry both sensory and motor signals. They are the vagus, the trigeminal, the facial, and the glossopharyngeal.

DiscoveryFact™

If all the nerves in the body were taken out and joined end to end, they would stretch about 60 miles.

Some people with spinal injuries use wheelchairs to move around.

Spinal cord

The 25th main nerve, the spinal cord, is the brain's chief link to the rest of the body. It starts at the brain stem and passes down into the body via a tunnel along the inside of the backbone. The bones of the spinal column protect the spinal cord from injury.

Spinal injury

An injury to the neck or back can damage the spinal cord, which may no longer carry signals between the brain and body parts. If the damage is low in the back, it can affect feeling and movement in the legs. If the damage is in the neck, then the arms may also lose feeling and movement.

Giant nerves

The squid's main nerve cell has a giant axon—a huge nerve fiber as thick as the lead in a pencil. This can easily be studied, cut, joined, and altered to find out how nerves work, how they carry nerve signals, and how they can repair themselves.

The squid is very useful for studying how nerves work.

Did you know?

- **Nerve signals travel along the nerves at speeds of up to 400 feet per second.**
- **The largest nerves can handle about 300 signals every single second.**
- **A person with a spinal injury who has lost the use of his or her legs is called a paraplegic, while someone who has lost the use of both arms and legs is called a quadriplegic.**

Quick Quiz

Are these sentences TRUE or FALSE?
Place the correct sticker in the box.

1. At birth, the body is only 4 percent of its adult size.
2. The bigger your brain, the smarter you are.
3. The cortex is the major site for thinking and for general awareness.
4. Nerve signals travel along the nerves at speeds of up to 400 feet per second.
5. If all the nerves in the body were taken out and joined end to end, they would stretch about 600 miles.

Find the stickers to finish the diagram.

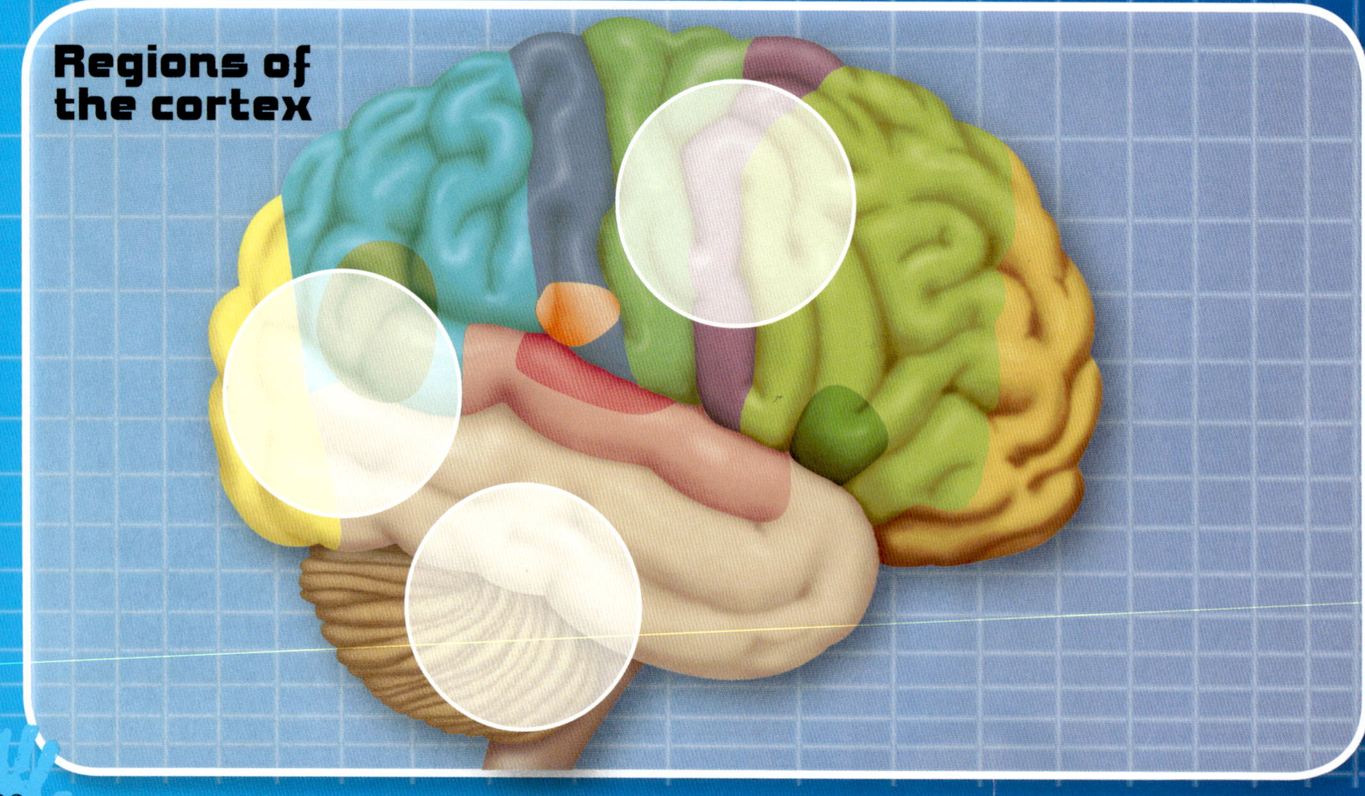

ANSWERS: 1 – T, 2 – F, 3 – T, 4 – T, 5 – F

The senses

Can you remember an exciting event such as an amusement park ride, circus, or music show? Take a moment to recall the bright lights, the sounds of the people, machines, and music, and the things you touched. You might also remember the different smells that were in the air and perhaps the taste of a snack or treat. Your body's sensory systems—sight, hearing, smell, taste, and touch—allow you to experience all these wonderful things.

The eyes

It is thought that over half of the information in our brains comes through our eyes—as words, photographs, drawings, real-life scenes, and images on screens.

DiscoveryFact™

The eye grows less than any other body part from birth to adulthood. It is already about 70 percent of its adult size at birth. This is why babies seem to have such big eyes.

Ball and socket

Each eyeball is protected by an orbit, or eye socket—a cone-shaped cavity in the skull. The eyeball is ball-shaped and measures about 1 inch across. Only about one-eighth of the eyeball is visible at the front.

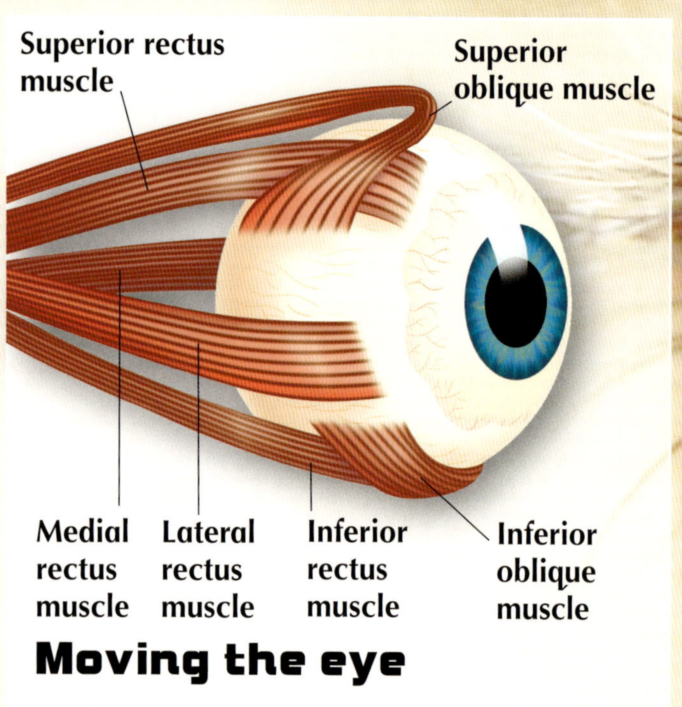

Moving the eye

Six long, slim, ribbonlike muscles join to different parts of the eyeball. Working as a team, these move the eyeball to look up or down and left or right. The eye muscles are among the fastest-reacting in the body.

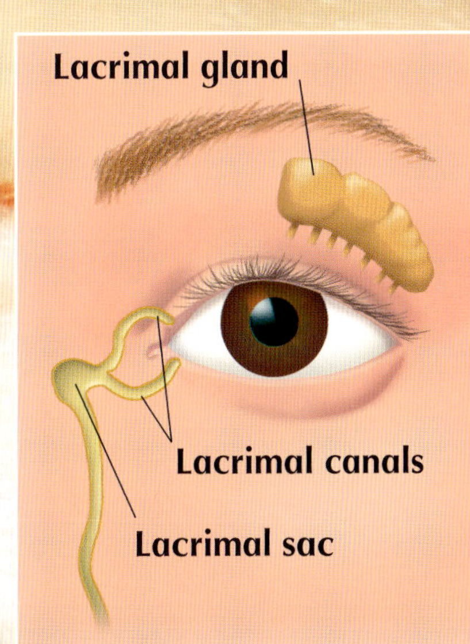

Making tears

Tear fluid is made in the lacrimal glands above each eyeball. Tears smear over the surface of the eyeball with each blink and wash away dust and germs. They then flow through two tubes to a pouch called the lacrimal sac and into the nose.

A crying baby

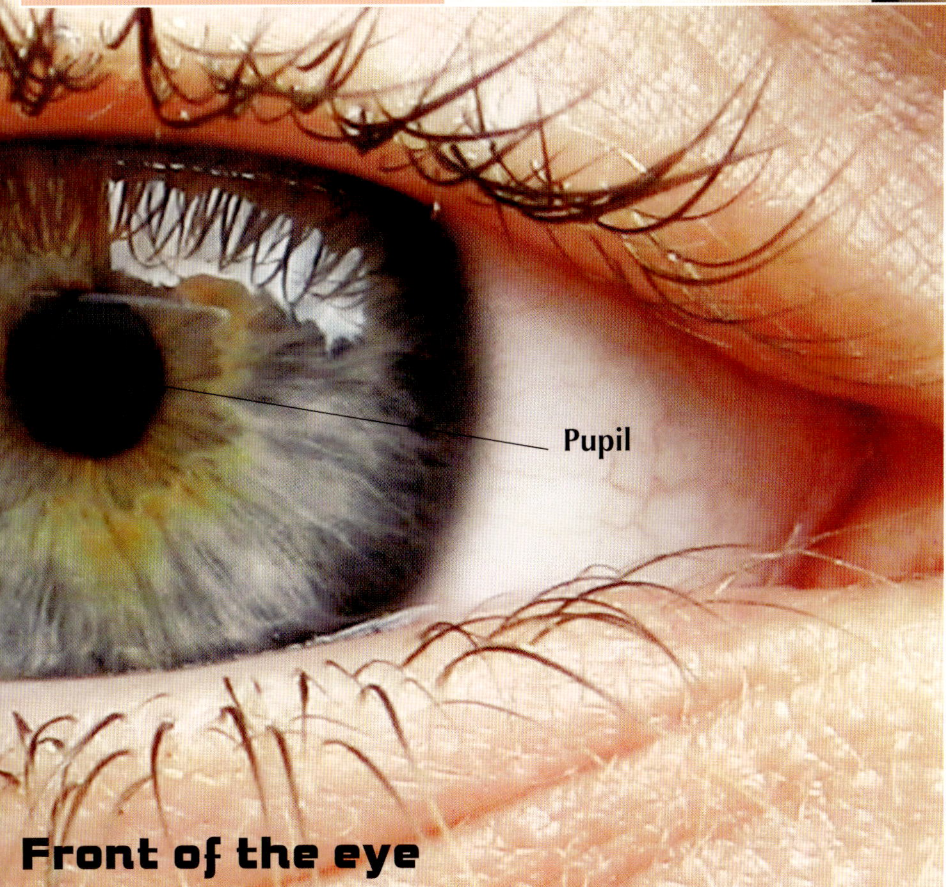

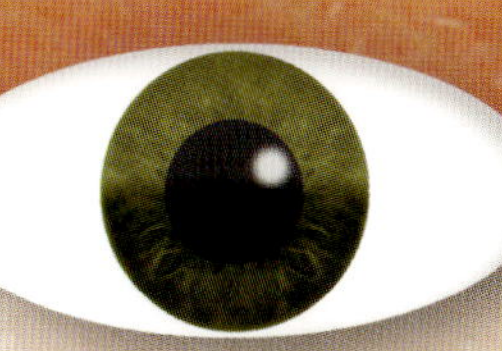

Normal light

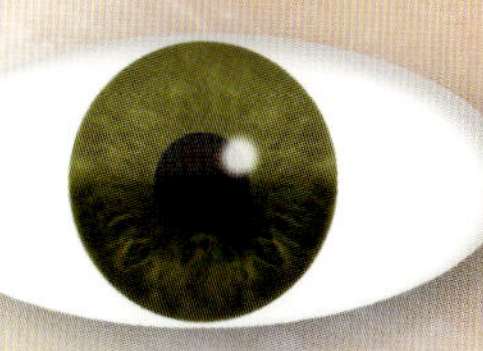

Bright light

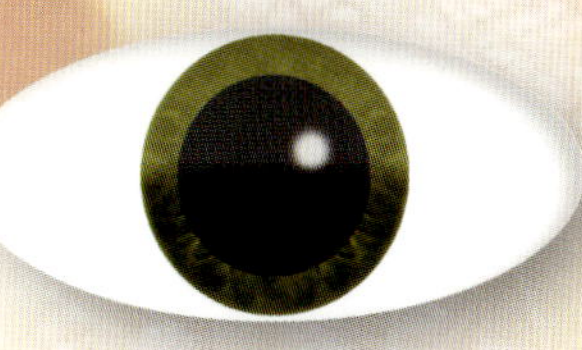

Dim light

Pupil response

The muscles of the iris relax or contract to change the size of the pupil. It widens in dim light to let in as much light as possible. In bright light, the pupil narrows to prevent too much light from entering.

Front of the eye

The most noticeable part of the eye is a ring of muscle called the iris, which varies in color from person to person. In the middle is the pupil, which looks like a black dot but is actually a hole that lets light into the eye's interior. Around the iris is the white of the eye—a tough outer covering of the eyeball called the sclera.

The ears

We do not hear with the ears on the sides of our head. These are simply flaps of skin and cartilage. Sounds are changed to nerve signals by a part inside the ear called the cochlea.

VIEW OF THE OUTER, MIDDLE AND INNER EAR

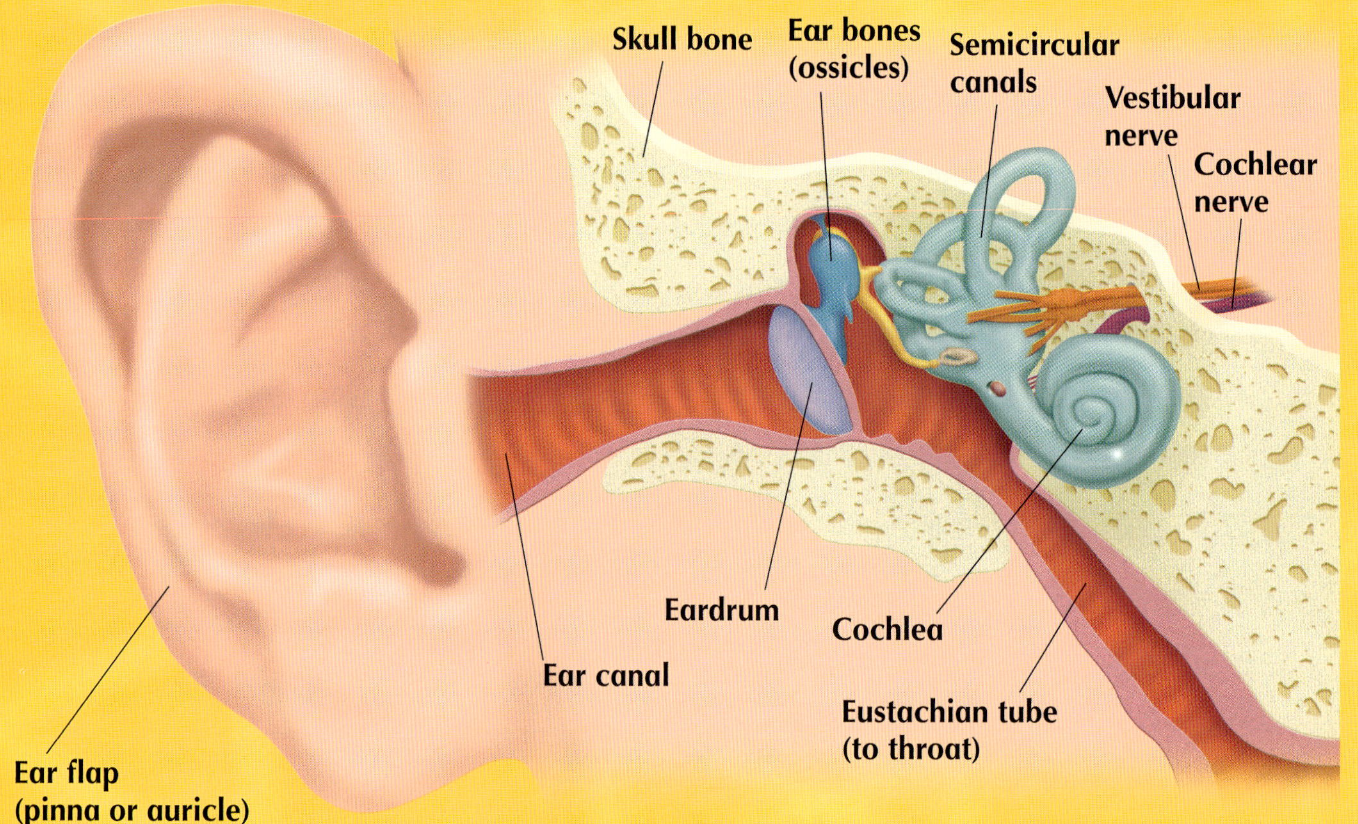

Ear flaps

The ear flaps help to gather sound waves from the air and guide them into the ear canal. Their shape also helps to keep dust, dirt, and other objects out of the ear. The canal's lining of wax also traps dust.

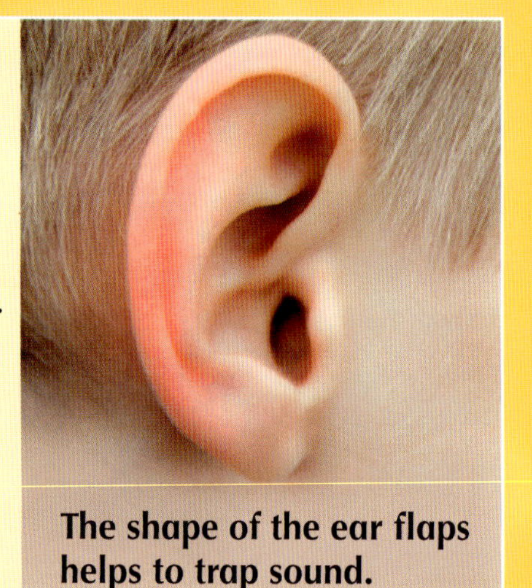

The shape of the ear flaps helps to trap sound.

Parts of the ear

The ear has three main sections. The outer ear is the ear flap on the side of the head and a tube—the ear canal—leading from it. The middle ear is the eardrum at the end of the ear canal and three tiny ear bones. The inner ear is the snail-like cochlea and the semicircular canals.

Look in the ear

Doctors can check for ear infections or other problems by shining a light from an otoscope into the ear canal. The ear lobe is usually pulled gently to make the ear canal straighter, to reveal the eardrum with the ear bones behind it.

A doctor uses an otoscope to check inside the ear.

DiscoveryFact™

Some animals, such as dogs and bats, can hear sounds that humans cannot detect. Some dog whistles seem to make no noise, but dogs can hear them!

Noticing sounds

Almost nowhere is truly silent. There are usually sounds of some kind: distant traffic, humming machinery, people talking, birds singing, or the wind. Much of the time we ignore these sounds because they tell us nothing new. The ears receive them, but our conscious thoughts do not register them. Only when we hear something new, important, or exciting do we turn our attention to listening.

A bat-eared fox has huge ear flaps, which it uses to locate insects to eat.

Direction of sound

Many animals have large ears that can turn to locate a sound. Humans work out the direction of a sound by hearing if the sound is louder on one side of the head than the other, and if a sound arrives at one ear before the other.

Did you know?

- **A sound's pitch—whether it sounds high or low—is measured in hertz.**
- **Human ears can hear a range of sounds, from low sounds at about 25 hertz to very high sounds at about 20,000 hertz.**

Nose and smell

Smell and taste are both known as chemosenses. This means that they detect chemical substances in the form of tiny particles too small to see. The nose reacts to smelly particles, called odorants, floating in the air.

Sniff, sniff

Odorant particles floating in the air drift into the nose as air is breathed in. They are detected by two olfactory patches in the roof of the nasal chamber. Sniffing something makes air swirl around inside the nose, which brings more odorant particles higher into the nasal chamber, where they touch the olfactory patches.

A flower produces odorant particles to attract insects so that it can pollinate.

DiscoveryFact™

The human nose is so sensitive that it can tell the difference between about 10,000 different scents.

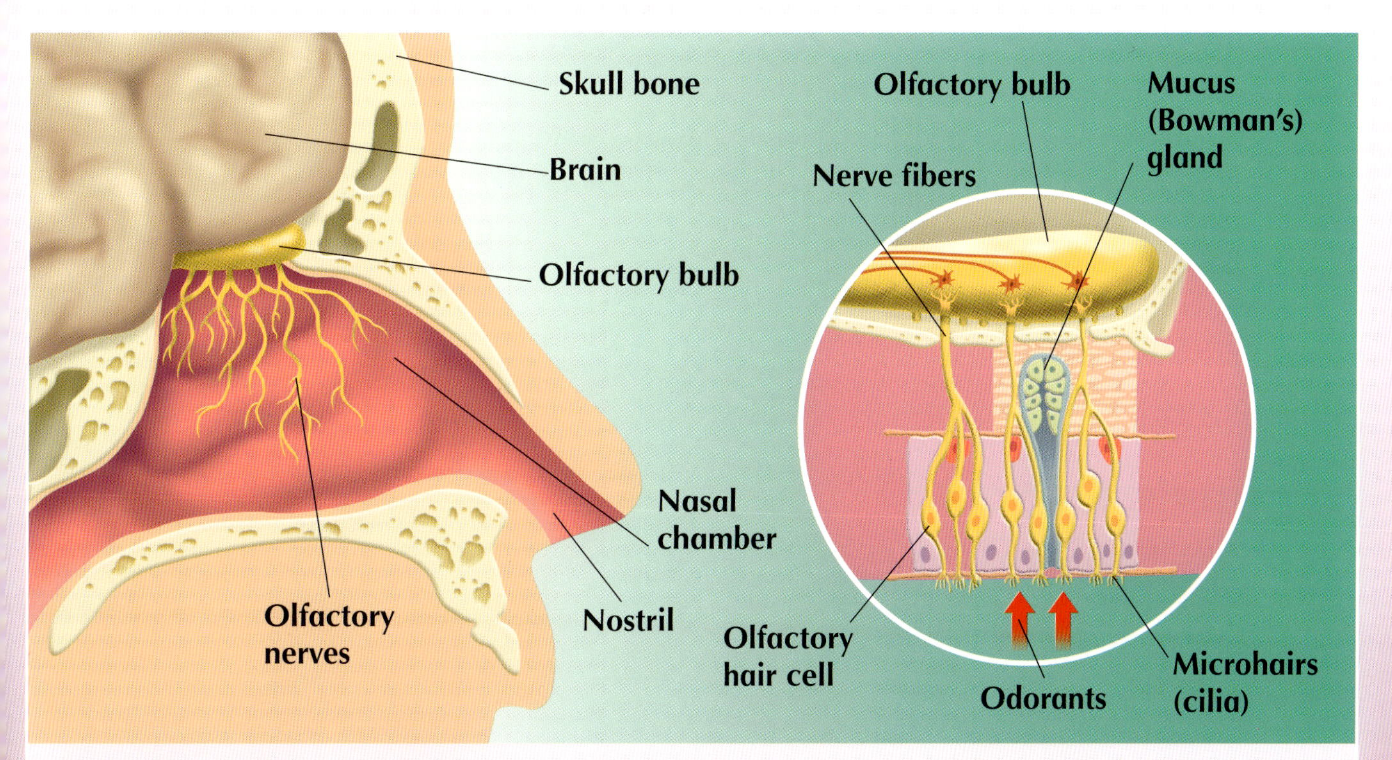

A close-up of an olfactory patch, where smells are turned into nerve signals

Inside the nose

The two nostrils lead into the nasal chamber—the air space inside the nose. Each olfactory patch in the roof of the nasal chamber contains about 10 million olfactory hair cells. These hair cells have about 10 to 20 microhairs each. The microhairs point down into the thick layer of slimy mucus that lines the inside of the nasal chamber.

Smell receptors

Odorant particles seep into the mucus coating the nasal chamber. They come into contact with the microhairs of the olfactory hair cells, and these create nerve signals. The signals are sent to the brain via the olfactory bulb. The brain interprets these signals as the aromas we smell.

Useful smells

The brain matches a smell to information it has stored about smells. For example, a wine taster can tell what type of wine he or she is about to drink just by sniffing it—they can even tell the year it was made.

A wine taster smells wine.

Tongue and taste

The tongue works in a similar way to the nose. It detects substances called flavorants in foods and drinks, using tiny taste buds located in bumps called papillae on its surface.

DiscoveryFact™

Over the years, some taste buds die and are not replaced. This means that younger people are more sensitive to taste than older people.

Tongue's surface

The tongue has groups of small, pimplelike papillae on its surface, which make it rough so that it can grip food. The largest ones are vallate papillae at the rear of the tongue. Other types are the long foliate papillae, the threadlike filiform papillae, and the mushroom-shaped fungiform papillae.

Taste buds

Scattered along the upper sides, tip, and back of the tongue are about 10,000 taste buds. Each contains 20 to 30 gustatory (taste) hair cells, whose microhairs stick up into a taste pore in the tongue's surface. Flavorants attach to these hairs and make the hair cells produce nerve signals.

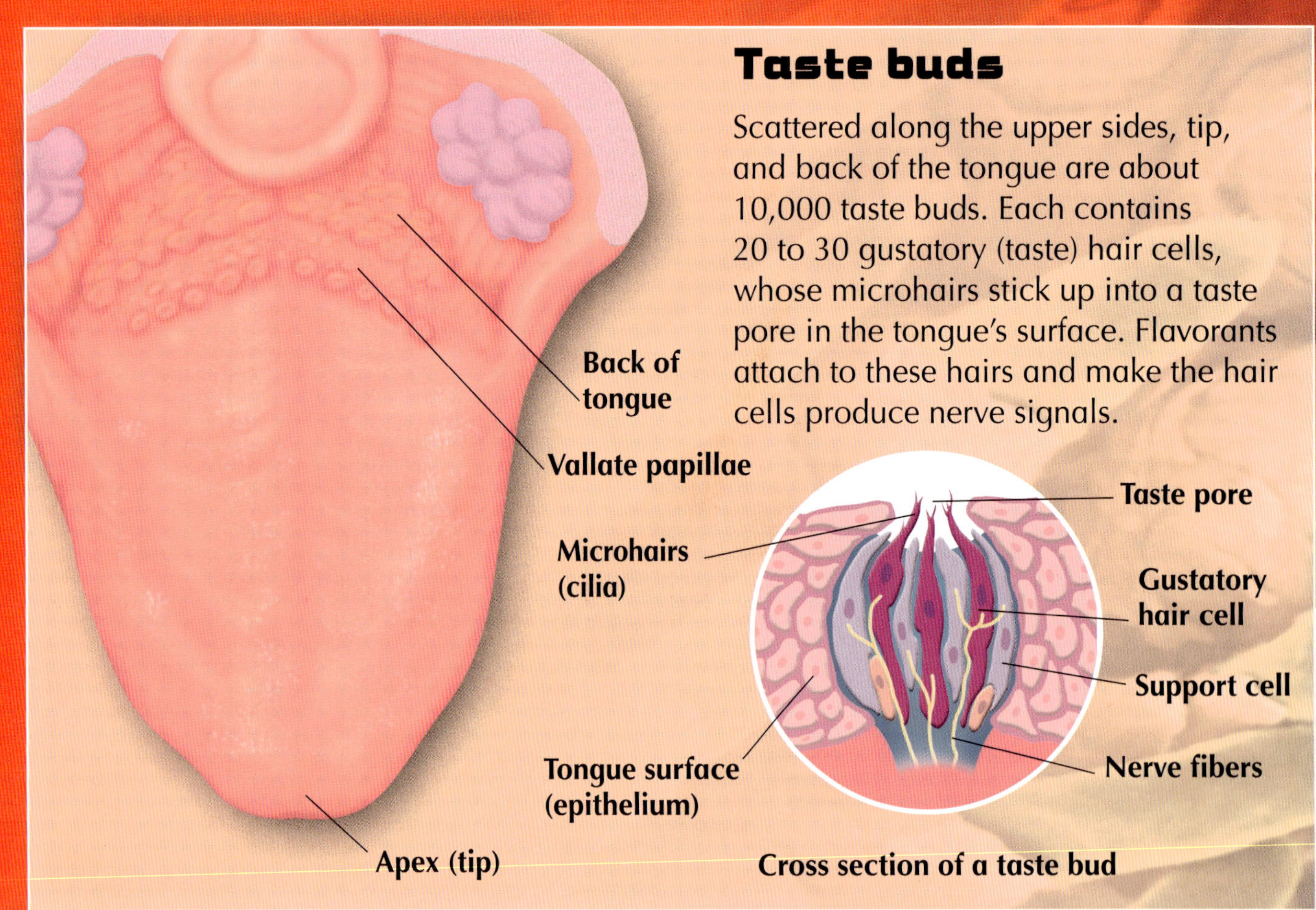

Cross section of a taste bud

Tasting food

The taste buds work in a similar way to the olfactory patches in the nose. They send nerve signals to the gustatory center in the brain (see page 78), which works out what flavor you are tasting. Your senses of taste and smell work together to determine the flavor. If you have a cold that has blocked your nose, you may notice that the food seems to have less taste. It has the same taste, but less smell, and so less overall flavor.

Vallate papilla

Magnified view of tongue papillae

Filiform papilla

Strong flavors

You can sense many different flavors. These are usually grouped into five categories—sweet, salt, sour, bitter, and savory (also called umami)—but there may be more, including spicy flavors such as those found in chilies.

Chilies produce a chemical that burns the tongue.

New thinking

For many years, it was thought that different parts of the tongue sensed different flavors. Recent research shows that most parts of the tongue detect most flavors, except for the central part of the tongue, which has no taste buds.

Quick Quiz

Are these sentences TRUE or FALSE? Place the correct sticker in the box.

1. The eyeball is the only organ that stays the same size from birth to adulthood.
2. The iris varies in color from person to person.
3. The ear has three main sections.
4. The human nose can tell the difference between about 100 different scents.
5. Our tongues have about 10,000 taste buds.

Find the stickers to finish the diagram.

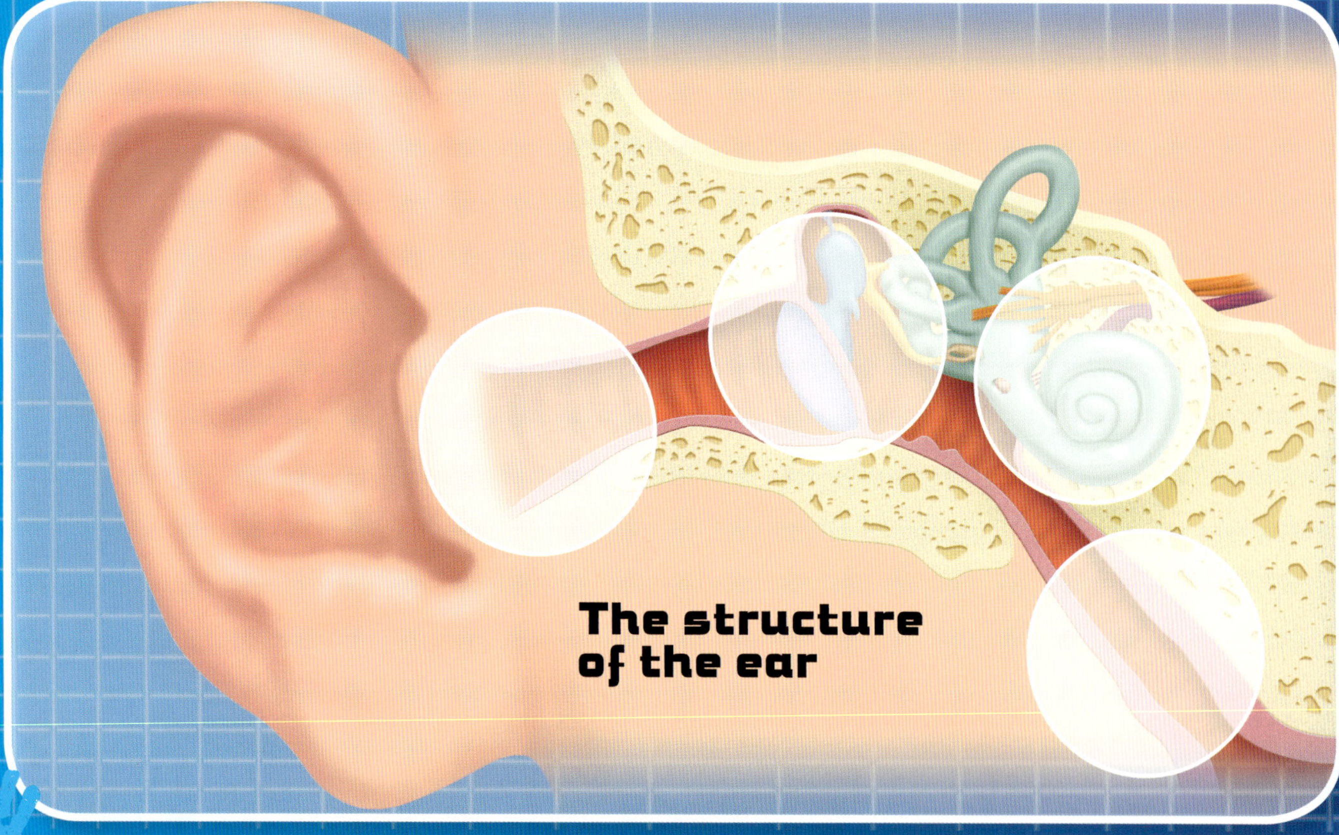

The structure of the ear

ANSWERS: 1 – F, 2 – T, 3 – T, 4 – F, 5 – T

Index

Index

Achilles tendon 26
Adam's apple 38
adenoids 34
airways 32, 37
albinism 11
alveoli 40, 41
amino acids 61
animals 8, 11, 17, 29, 59, 63, 81, 87
anus 58, 69
arteries 46, 47, 48, 50, 51, 54, 55, 73
artificial respiration 43
axons 76, 77, 79, 81

babies 23, 62, 69, 84
biceps 27
biting 62, 63
blood 12, 45, 49, 61, 67
blood cells 12, 13, 23, 52 53, 68
blood clots 12, 13, 53
blood donors 53
blood flow 47, 48, 50–51
blood groups 53
blood pressure 47, 54, 55, 75
blood transfusion 53
blood vessels 9, 12, 22, 35, 40, 45, 46, 51, 54–55, 63
bone marrow 22, 23
bones 20-25, 61
brain 42, 43, 50, 58, 71, 72–75, 76, 77, 78–79, 80, 84, 89
brain injury 73
brain stem 58, 75
brain waves 77
breathing 31, 32–35, 38, 39, 41, 42–43, 75, 80
breathing muscles 27, 33, 42–43
breathing rate 43
bronchi and bronchioles 32, 40
bruises 12

cancellous (spongy) bone 22, 23
canines 62, 63
capillaries 41, 50, 54
carbohydrates 61, 67
carbon dioxide 41, 42, 45
carotid artery 50
cartilage 24, 34, 36, 38, 40
cerebellum 75
cerebral cortex 74, 78, 79
cerebrospinal fluid 72
cerebrum 72, 74, 78
chambers 48–49, 72, 75
chemosenses 88
choking 37
circulatory (cardiovascular) system 45–55
cochlea 21, 86
collagen 22
colon 68, 69
compact bone 22
coronary arteries 46, 47
corpus callosum 75
cranial nerves 80
cranium 72, 73
cuticle 16
cuts and wounds 12–13, 53

defecation 69
dendrites 11, 76, 77
dentine 63
dermis 8, 9
diaphragm 33, 42, 43
digestion 57, 58–59, 64–69, 75
digestive tract 58, 59, 68
duodenum 64, 66

ear 21, 26, 79, 86–87
ear flaps 86
echocardiogram 48
emotions 28, 29, 74, 75
enamel 62, 63
enzymes 64, 65, 66, 67
epidermis 8, 12, 14
epiglottis 36, 38
erythrocytes 52
esophagus (gullet) 36, 40, 58, 64, 65, 67
expressions 28, 29
eye 11, 79, 84–85
eyebrow 28, 29

face masks 35
facial muscles 28–29
feces 68, 69
fiber 61, 68
fibrin 12, 13
fingerprints 8
flavors 91
food 36, 37, 57, 58–61, 64, 65, 68
frowning 28, 29
fungal infection 17

gastric pits 65
germs 8, 12, 13, 34, 36, 37 53
glottis 38
gustatory center 78, 91

hair 7, 8, 11, 14–15, 34
hair cells 14, 15, 89, 90
hair follicles 14, 15
hamstrings 27
healthy diet 60
hearing 79, 86–87
heart 45, 46–49, 54, 55
heart attack 47
heart muscle 46, 47
heartburn 65
height 21
Heimlich maneuver 37
hemophilia 13
hinge joints 24

hole in the heart 49
hydrochloric acid 65
hypothalamus 58, 74, 75, 79

ileum 66
incisors 62, 63

inferior vena cava 46, 50, 54
integumentary system 8
intelligence 75
intercostal muscles 33, 42, 43
intestines 58, 61, 64, 66–69

jejunum 66
joints 19, 24–25

keratin 16, 17

lacrimal glands 85
large intestine 66, 67, 68–69
larynx (voice box) 27, 32, 36, 38–39
leukocytes 53
lipase 65
liver 59, 66, 67
lobes 40, 74, 78
lungs 27, 32, 33, 34, 37, 40 41, 42, 43, 48, 51
lymph 67

melanin 10, 11
melanocytes 10, 11
meninges 72
microbes 68
mind 79
molars and premolars 62, 63
motor nerves 76, 80
motor skills 78
MRI (magnetic resonanc imaging) 73
mucosa 64, 65
mucus 34, 65, 68, 89
muscles 14, 19, 20, 26–29, 39, 46, 51, 54, 55, 64, 80
myelin sheath 76

nails 7, 8, 16–17
nasal cavity 32, 33, 34, 35, 36, 88, 89
nerve cells 71, 76, 77, 78, 79
nerve signals 75, 76–77, 81, 86, 89
nerves 9, 22, 71, 75, 80–81
nervous system 71–81
neurons 76
neurotransmitters 77
nose 33, 34–35, 42, 88–89
nosebleed 35
nostrils 34, 89
nutrients 47, 50, 52, 63, 67, 68

olfactory patches 88, 89
oxygen 31, 32, 40, 41, 42, 43, 45, 46, 47, 49, 50, 51, 52

palate 34
pancreas 59, 66
papillae 90, 91
pepsin 65
personality 79
pharynx 36, 38
plasma 52
platelets 12, 13, 23, 52, 53
processed foods 61
pronunciation 39
proteins 61, 65, 67
pulmonary arteries 46, 48
pulmonary circulation 51
pupil 85

rectum 68, 69
respiration see breathing
respiratory center 42

scabs 12, 13, 53
scars 13
sebaceous glands 15
sebum 15, 17
senses 78, 80, 83–91
sight 79, 84–85
sinuses 34, 35, 39
skeletal muscles 26, 27
skeleton 20–21, 23
skin 7, 8–13, 15
skin cells 8
skin color 10–11
skull 20, 23, 25, 35, 72
small intestine 66, 67
smell, sense of 33, 88–89, 91
smiling 29
smooth muscle 54, 55
sounds 27, 38–39, 87
sphincters 64
spinal cord 81
spinal injury 81
stomach 36, 58, 64–65, 66, 67
stomach wall 64
stroke 49, 73
sunburn 11
sunscreen 10
suntan 10
superior vena cava 46, 50, 54
swallowing 36, 37, 58
sweat 9, 59
swimming 27, 35
synapses 77
systemic arteries 50
systemic circulation 50, 51

taste 90–91
taste buds 90, 91
tears 85
teeth 39, 62–63
thalamus 74, 75, 79
throat 32, 36–37, 58
thrombocytes 53
tongue 39, 90–91
tonsils 36, 37

valves 47, 48, 54
varicose veins 54
vascular network 50
veins 46, 47, 50, 51, 54, 55
ventricles 48, 49, 72, 75
villi 66, 67
vitamins and minerals 22, 23, 61
vocal cords 38, 39

waste products 45, 50, 52, 58, 59, 68, 69
water 59, 68
windpipe 32, 36, 37, 42, 43
wisdom teeth 63

Acknowledgments

Artwork supplied through the Art Agency by Terry Pastor, Barry Croucher, Robin Carter, and Dave Smith

Photo credits:
b = bottom, bk = back, c = center, r = right, l = left, t = top

Front cover tc iStock/Sebastian Kaulitzki, tbk iStock, bl Rod Ferris/Dreamstime.com, c Micro Discovery/Corbis, bbk Visuals Unlimited/Corbis, bc iStock
Back cover bl Mehaykulyk/Science Photo Library

1 Linda Bucklin/Dreamstime.com, 2–3 75 Zena Holloway/zefa/Corbis, 6–7 Micro Discovery/Corbis, 8–9 William Attard Mccarthy/Dreamstime.com, 8cl Anette Linnea Rasmussen/Dreamstime.com, 8cr Dreamstime.com, 9tl Pierre Lahalle/TempSport/Corbis, 10–11 Gabe Palmer/zefa/Corbis, 10l Dreamstime.com, 11tr Dreamstime.com, 12–13 Visuals Unlimited/Corbis, 13tr Reuters/CORBIS, 14–15 Anthony Redpath/CORBIS, 15tr Mediscan/Corbis, 15bl Dreamstime.com, 16–17 Fendis/zefa/Corbis, 17tr Visuals Unlimited/Corbis, 17bl Anke Van Wyk/Dreamstime.com, 19 Visuals Unlimited/Corbis, 20tc Dreamstime.com, 21bl Bettmann/CORBIS, 22–23 and 23bl Lester V. Bergman/CORBIS, 22cl Lester V. Bergman/CORBIS, 24–25 Duomo/CORBIS, 24bl all Dreamstime.com, 25cr Dreamstime.com, 25bc Dreamstime.com, 26–27 Linda Bucklin/Dreamstime.com, 26 Janet Carr/Dreamstime.com, 27tc Oleg Kozlov/Dreamstime.com, 27cr Rod Ferris/Dreamstime.com, 28–29 Linda Bucklin/Dreamstime.com, 28bl Dreamstime.com 29tr Jurie Maree/Dreamstime.com, 31 Ben Welsh/zefa/Corbis, 32cl Graça Victoria/Dreamstime.com, 32br Dreamstime.com, 33tr Jaimie Duplass/Dreamstime.com, 33b Katrina Brown/Dreamstime.com, 34–35 Dreamstime.com, 35tr Pete Saloutos/zefa/Corbis, 35br David Badenhorst/Dreamstime.com, 36–37 Najlah Feanny/Corbis, 37tr Lester V. Bergman/CORBIS, 38–39 Robbie Jack/Corbis, 39c Howard Sandler Dreamstime.com, 40–41 Visuals Unlimited/Corbis, 41tr Lester V. Bergman/CORBIS, 43tr Sonya Etchison/Dreamstime.com, 43br Roman Milert/Dreamstime.com, 45 Visuals Unlimited/Corbis, 46cl Ioana Grecu/Dreamstime.com, 47bl Howard Sochurek/CORBIS, 50tl Tim Pannell/Corbis, 50–51 Dreamstime.com, 51bl Galina Barskaya/Dreamstime.com, 52–53 Sebastian Kaulitzki/Dreamstime.com, 53tr Dreamstime.com, 53br Wa Li/Dreamstime.com, 54–55 Wa Li/Dreamstime.com, 57 Klaus Hackenberg/zefa/Corbis, 58r Dreamstime.com, 59cr Jason Stitt/Dreamstime.com, 59bc Gert Vrey/Dreamstime.com, 60r Olga Lyubkina/Dreamstime.com, 61tr Dreamstime.com, 61cr Ryan Pike/Dreamstime.com, 61bc Nicolas Nadjar/Dreamstime.com, 62l Linda Bucklin/Dreamstime.com, 62br Paul Moore/Dreamstime.com, 63br Dreamstime.com, 64–65 and 65tl Lester V. Bergman/CORBIS, 65tr Dreamstime.com, 65bl Howard Sochurek/CORBIS, 66–67 Micro Discovery/Corbis, 68–69 Dreamstime.com, 69t Howard Sochurek/CORBIS, 69br Dreamstime.com, 71 Lester V. Bergman/CORBIS, 73tr Ronnie Kaufman/CORBIS, 73cl Verett Kennedy Brown/epa/Corbis, 73bc Dreamstime.com, 74 Bob Rowan; Progressive Image/CORBIS, 74cl Dreamstime.com, 75tr Roger Bruce/Dreamstime.com, 75bl Dreamstime.com, 76bl Kamil fazrin Rauf/Dreamstime.com, 77tl Yves Forestier/CORBIS SYGMA, 77cr Richard T. Nowitz/CORBIS, 79tl Doconnell/Dreamstime.com, 79tr Dreamstime.com, 79bl Loke Yek Mang/Dreamstime.com, 80–81 Asther Lau Choon Siew/Dreamstime.com, 81tl Alistair Scott/Dreamstime.com, 81bl Ilya Gridnev/Dreamstime.com, 83 Visuals Unlimited/Corbis, 84–85 Dreamstime.com, 85tr Dreamstime.com, 86bc Gordana Sermek/Dreamstime.com, 87t Dreamstime.com, 87bl Vladimir Pomortsev/Dreamstime.com, 88bl Daniel Gustavsson/Dreamstime.com, 89br Franz Pfluegl/Dreamstime.com, 90–91 Visuals Unlimited/Corbis, 91br Milan Kopcok/Dreamstime.com, 93tc Dreamstime.com, 93br Yanik Chauvin/Dreamstime.com